D1286892

Savory Memories

Savory Memories

L. Elisabeth Beattie, Editor

∾

Illustrations by Elisabeth Watts Beattie

With a Foreword by Ronni Lundy
and an Afterword by Jim Wayne Miller

∾

THE UNIVERSITY PRESS OF KENTUCKY

Publication of this volume was made possible in part
by a grant from the National Endowment for the Humanities.

Scholarly publisher for the Commonwealth,
serving Bellarmine College, Berea College, Centre
College of Kentucky, Eastern Kentucky University,
The Filson Club Historical Society, Georgetown College,
Kentucky Historical Society, Kentucky State University,
Morehead State University, Murray State University,
Northern Kentucky University, Transylvania University,
University of Kentucky, University of Louisville,
and Western Kentucky University.

Editorial and Sales Offices: The University Press of Kentucky
663 South Limestone Street, Lexington, Kentucky 40508-4008

98 99 00 01 02 5 4 3 2 1

Library of Congress Cataloging-in-Publication Data

Savory memories / L. Elisabeth Beattie, editor ;
illustrations by Elisabeth Watts Beattie ; with a foreword by
Ronni Lundy and an afterword by Jim Wayne Miller.
p.   cm.
ISBN 0-8131-2046-2
1. Cookery, American. 2. Authors, American—Kentucky
—Anecdotes. I. Beattie, L. Elisabeth, 1953-
TX715.S274   1998
641.5973—dc21   97-32708

This book is printed on acid-free recycled paper
meeting the requirements of the American National Standard
for Permanence of Paper for Printed Library Materials.

Manufactured in the United States of America

To my mother,
Elisabeth Morton Watts Beattie,
who has nourished me—
body and soul—for four decades,
and whose book this is more than mine,
and to the memory of my maternal grandmother,
Iva Hensley Watts,
whose hugs and Sunday dinners
highlighted my Missouri childhood

with love

Contents

Foreword

"If, beyond the pearly gates, I am permitted to select my place at the table, it will be among Kentuckians." The first time I laid eyes on these words from historian Thomas D. Clark, they struck me as gospel. For me there will be no heaven unless it is laid out around a round oak table turned oblong by company's-coming leaves and stretched into infinity to accommodate those who have gathered joyfully, eagerly, around Kentucky tables here on earth.

At this table I will, of course, find the relatives and family friends who nourished and nurtured me as a child. My Aunt Ariel will be presiding over the world's finest jam cake while Aunt Johnny slips me a handful of red and yellow "tommytoes," still warm from the garden whose earth I can smell on her chapped but tender fingers. Charlie, my favorite uncle, will be crouched to the side, laughing and goading Daddy on to crank, crank, crank that freezer of homemade ice cream. And Ethel will be passing a big bowl of milky creamed corn, scraped from ears my Uncle Clifton has raised, and the perfect match for Jessie's white half-runner beans cooked long and slow to tender perfection.

There will be no rank strangers there—not for me nor for anyone who cares to join us. As has been the custom throughout Kentucky's history, the table of my home state will always have room for anyone who is hungry, and enough food to be divided up and shared until everyone there is fed.

How will you find us? Well, I'm afraid we will likely be the noisiest table in heaven. You can follow your nose to the source of the tangy, sweet scent of cornbread baking in seasoning-slicked cast-iron pans, but just as surely, you can follow your ears to the cacophony of never-ending conversation punctuated by whoops of laughter. Here is what Clark goes on to say in *The Kentucky* (1942): "Eating dinner in Kentucky is more than a physiological refueling of the human body, it is a joyous social ritual. The table is the great yarning place for the state. Gossip, tall yarns, and laughter punctuate the business at hand of consuming victuals. This, to the Kentuckian, is his great 'recalling ground.' He drags out his salty little family secrets and laughs about them. A warning to all strangers, however: the family secrets are never quite so secretive or so outrageous as they appear on the surface. There is something about a Kentucky dinner that stretches a yarn or puts spirit into a bit of gossip."

And what if you can't wait for that great, bright, glorious feast up yonder? Then grab yourself a long spoon and a tall glass of crumble-in and curl up someplace comfortable with this book right now.

In these pages you will find just the sort of frank and funny, sometimes raucous, always revealing tales that good food has eternally accompanied at Kentucky tables. We are writers by profession, those of us gathered around the textual table here, but we are storytellers by birth and raising. And while this collection of food memories and reminiscences from the likes of Michael Dorris, George Ella Lyon, Betty Layman Receveur, Ed McClanahan, and more is marked by deft craftsmanship, the stories here are distinguished even more by their intimate, conversational voices. We're not writing at you, friend, but simply talking with you around the table.

In these stories we talk about pain and beauty, love, fear, religion, writing, the sense of belonging and of being cast out. The tales here explore territory from the limitless imagination of a child to the limits of death, then beyond. We remember foolishness and fancy, sidle up to facts that are too hard to look at head on, discover truth all unexpected when we were only looking for something good to eat. We remember those who loved us and showed it by nourishment. With every bite we come closer to telling you—to knowing ourselves—who we are, who and where it is we've come from, and, sometimes, sometimes, where it is we must go.

That all of these stories have as their spark and substance a memory of food is no literary artifice.

Food may be the greatest mnemonic device of all. John Egerton reminds us that it strikes all the senses at once, and so a memory can suddenly spring full blown from the simple scent of cut oranges or cinnamon toast, or from the soothing texture of warm grits on the tongue. The colors of food become standards for the mind's palette: cherry red, lemon yellow, avocado green. The flavors can instantly transport us through time and space. And there are the sounds of the foods themselves—the snap and crunch of a bite from the first vine-picked cucumber of the season—and of their preparation. ("How do you know when it's time to take the lid off a skillet of fried chicken?" someone once asked a Kentucky cook. "Honey," she said, "You know that sound it makes just when the grease comes down off the inside of the lid—moving all across, just like a waterfall? When it does that, it's ready.")

I need only hear a metal spoon being stirred slowly around the bottom of a skillet and I am back in my mother's kitchen, small and sleepy-eyed, waiting for the chipped beef and gravy she will feed my father before he goes off to the night shift at the distillery and I go off to bed. I need only hear that sound and I can see the muted yellow glow from the lamp above the sink, taste the salt of the beef, feel the crunch of the toast, and I am in the safe and loving arms of my parents once again.

It is not simply that the food reminds us of a bigger, more significant memory, but that so often food is the signifier in the memory itself. So it is that the spaghetti sauce of Dianne Aprile's paternal grandmother becomes the battleground where her mother and grandmother struggle over whose imprint will triumph in succeeding generations. And Martha Bennett Stiles's mother's maypop jelly, fried puffballs, chickweed salads, and Innisfree Rock (fish) become the art studies she left behind and a delicious link between past and present.

For Alexander "Sandy" Speer, his Grandmother's Baked Chicken is truth incarnate and brings a lesson he never forgets about the shame of lies. And for Lee Pennington, the ritual of making snow cream honors the goodness of his mother and the magical, sacred moment "when angels comb their hair."

For some—especially those who believe that history (both personal and global) can only be told in terms of battles won and territories lost—the idea of a clutch of serious writers writing about food may seem a playful exercise at best. But for those of us raised up in Kentucky, in the combined ritual of the tale and the table, there is an instinctive understanding that such writing—about food, nourishment, need, and the ways we fill it—is the closest to truth we get.

M.F.K. Fisher said: "There is a community of more than our bodies when bread is broken and wine is drunk. And that is my answer when people ask me: Why do you write about hunger, and not wars and love?"

I am always surprised that she never made her home in Kentucky.

Guy Davenport, who has, wrote: "Eating is the most intimate and at the same time the most public of biological functions. Going from dinner table to dinner table is the equivalent of going from one culture to another, even within the same family."

So come on in. Pull up a chair. Make that journey with us.

And would you like a little bite to eat?

Ronni Lundy

Preface

Four years ago I found myself impaneled with colleagues—all writers—addressing an audience at an annual meeting of the Kentucky Arts Council. We spoke about how our careers began—about how creativity and passion, mentors, and pure luck—launched us one by one into the magical world of words. We had each taken different paths to the same destination—a realm expansive enough to include poetry and prose, essays and criticism, biography, and even creative nonfiction. Our assembly attested shameless devotion to the vocation that sustains us—not always because we selected it but inevitably because it adopted us. Appraise any writer distracted too long from his or her craft and you will see determination in his eyes, purpose in her stride—an overall air of intent signaling a need to feed the soul.

And so at lunch that day our talk turned to food, the reality of the stuffed pita pockets and vegetable medleys before us serving as metaphors for our psychic cravings. Having recently concluded an exhilarating but exhausting round of interviews with authors for my first book, *Conversations With Kentucky Writers*, I turned to Betty Layman Receveur and in a facetious and, I hoped, droll tone said, "My next book should be a Kentucky writers' cookbook." Instead of arching her brows as I anticipated, Betty replied, "Actually, all my sons ever demand of me is my pound cake." Sena Jeter Naslund, seated to my right, chimed in, "And food imagery is so significant in my fiction!" Jim Wayne Miller, listening across the table, leaned closer, nodded, and smiled.

From the ingredients gathered at that meal a recipe emerged, an idea for a book of vignettes that would allow representative Kentucky writers to explore how their memories of relatives and food helped nurture their responses to life. My concept centered more on collecting expressive essays than on creating a balanced diet of entries, yet this completed work serves both as a cookbook and a compendium of sentiments, all dedicated to memories of relatives who helped shape the personas of the authors themselves.

So that's how this book emerged, with my requesting writers to transform raw experiences into epiphanous concoctions. The smorgasbord herein encompasses the ingredients and largesse of any family's reunion; the essays' tones range from bemused to reverent, their styles from flippant to elegiac. Together they harmonize as do families and meals at their best, the entries' disparate voices adding flavor and interest to their blended conversation.

It's true, I think, that the ideal flourishes most profoundly in memory and possibility. These essays allow us, their readers, to transcend time and place; they illustrate fresh approaches to extracting meaning from the present, yet ever elusive, moment. So dig in. Indulge. Sample and savor and linger at your leisure. The memories in this book are sometimes sweet and always poignant. The recipes are usually tasty, and occasionally edible only with tongue planted firmly in cheek. A toast to the authors who've prepared this repast. Lift a glass to their ancestors and to all of ours, too. For they are the people who first fed our needs. They are the grandparents and parents, aunts and uncles, brothers and sisters, friends and neighbors who in their accumulated wisdom and well-tested love led us all to partake at life's table.

Although I'll assume credit for conceiving this literary cornucopia, recognition for its fruition belongs to the Kentucky authors whose eloquent contributions appear herein, as well as to the artist—my mother, Elisabeth Watts Beattie—whose illustrations complement each essay.

Additional thanks go to Ronni Lundy for her elegant foreword and to the late Jim Wayne Miller for his articulate afterword.

Appreciation for her excellent typing skills and for her unwavering ability to meet emergency deadlines with gracious good will goes to Candy Jerdon, just as my gratitude for her daunting gifts as a proofreader and for her immeasurable value as a friend who insists on intellectual integrity goes to Marion Kingston Stocking.

I also extend my thanks to Elizabethtown Community College's administrators, especially President Charles E. Stebbins, Academic Dean Ty Handy, and Fine Arts and Humanities Division Chair Jimmie Bruce, as well as to Kentucky Community College System Chancellor Ben W. Carr Jr. and to the University of Kentucky Board of Trustees for granting me a sabbatical leave to complete this and other books.

And finally I offer my continuing appreciation to my parents, Elisabeth Watts Beattie and Walter Matthew Beattie Jr., for their psychic and financial support of this project.

The Shape of Comfort

Dianne Aprile

My son, Josh, believes there are really only two major food groups—
Italian and Jewish—and he belongs to both. For Josh, blood ancestry and
culinary lineage mingle and merge as naturally as basil and cheese in
pesto, or apples, almonds, and honey in charoses. To be Italian is to *mangia
pasta*. To be Jewish is to nosh on lox. A mixed birthright, to Josh's way of
thinking, is a passport to the best of both worlds.

Some will tell you, you are what you eat. Josh is proof you eat what
you are. Among his first solid foods were miniature green and red pillows
of ravioli pinched with dough made of spinach and tomato flour at our
neighborhood pasta shop. He cut his teeth on untoasted bagels and fist-

sized chunks of parmesan. Today he would be hard-pressed to tell you which he likes best, pepperoni or pastrami, though he knows which word is Italian and which only sounds so but in truth is pure Yiddish.

For Josh, food and family co-exist peacefully in childhood, nourishing and sustaining him, feeding not only his body but his soul, satisfying metaphoric needs as well as those of his gut.

For me, the balance was always trickier. I grew up with strong-willed, obstinate, embattled foods. Foods fraught with fear and jealousy as well as comfort and sustenance. Foods that demanded allegiance. Survivor foods. Taboo foods. Food as reminders of past sacrifice, offered on the holy altar of the dining room table.

The foods I remember are hearty, wholesome dishes; recipes that took time and concentration and much fretting and more prayer—but not a lot of expense or exotic-shopping time, and never ever a cookbook.

In these foods that I loved and still crave, I tasted the geography of two families, the bitter lands they left behind. Stingy fields of Ireland. Defeated villages of Sicily. No wonder that some bore the flavor of trouble, the bite of crushed hope.

I see the foods of my childhood in big stubborn pots clattering on the tops of stoves. They are women's foods for the most part. Food fussed over and nursed, fretted over and coaxed, feared and revered, and, sometimes by the foolish or the young among us, jeered.

Victoria's Meatballs

one and one-half pounds ground beef
eight ounces fine bread crumbs
one lightly beaten egg
one-fourth cup freshly grated parmesan
one-fourth cup warm water
three teaspoons (or less) salt
one-half teaspoon basil
one-fourth teaspoon pepper
two teaspoons oregano
garlic cloves, peeled and crushed

Mix and roll into balls. Brown in a pan. Add to homemade marinara sauce and simmer for four hours. Serves six.

My father was first-generation Italian-American. Both his parents came to Louisville as youngsters, leaving behind the customs and the cuisine of their isolated communities on the outskirts of Palermo, Sicily. My mother was mixed-breed—Irish, Swiss, and German—but the Irish is what left its stamp.

Despite quite similar strains of melancholy and regret running through my Irish and Sicilian family histories, there was, as far back as I can recall, a certain competition between the two heritages. This rivalry, however masked or muted in daily life, surfaced blatantly in the kitchen, especially at holiday time.

I can still see my grandmother, Victoria Giacalone Aprile, climbing our front steps to join us for dinner. It might be Mother's Day, or Christmas Day, or Thanksgiving. The dress might change, the purse, the haircut; but always she carried the same foil-wrapped, dishtowel-insulated steamy casserole dish.

My brothers and I both dreaded and delighted in the inevitable moment when my mother would peer through the folds of her organdy curtains and catch sight of my grandmother coming up those stairs in her lace-up, black leather "old lady" shoes, one step at a time, until she arrived at our door: shamelessly, notoriously, insistently meatball-laden. It was an affront to my mother somehow, this invasion of pasta and marinara, unwelcome foreign forces infiltrating her assiduously assimilated, all-American troops. Especially at holidays, it irked her: the sight of turkey, dressing, cranberries, green beans, mashed potatoes, gravy, . . . and meatballs?

My mother was not usually one to be so narrow-minded, so I sided with her in this controversy for years, out of habit, out of loyalty, even after my mother died and my grandmother (and her pasta) endured. It was when Victoria died and I began to collect the fragments of her personal history in hopes of making sense of her pessimism and mournfulness that I came to understand the significance of the food she brought to our table. Although we rolled our eyes and laughed at those red globes of ground beef and egg and basil, she was right to be uncompromising, to force upon us this token, this relic, of the life she'd left behind. Where would we be, the children of her oldest son, had she not left that life at the age of four and climbed the gangway of a ship, bearing one precious armload of baggage step by step as now she toted pasta and meatballs to our door?

My mother never adjusted to my grandmother's meatballs, or to her other kitchen quirks. For example, Grandma insisted on bringing her own chunk of cheese to grate into a bowl, turning up her nose at our glossy container of perfectly well-preserved Kraft parmesan. She called spaghetti "pasta," a quaint term in those days, and flatly refused to eat anything cooked with butter. The last laugh was hers, however. She was, as it turns out, a living testimony to the cholesterol-lowering properties of olive oil, which she used exclusively right up to her death at age ninety-seven when her heart, still vigorously pumping, was overruled by the rest of her worn-out body.

My mother saw Grandma's meatballs, rightly, as a fetish. They were her amulets, her protection from any further assault on her identity. As I came to understand later, Victoria's life in many ways exemplified the dark side of ethnic assimilation in turn-of-the-century America.

Some might explain away her sadness as emotional residue passed on to her from generations of Sicilian ancestors who were subjugated by landowners and nobility. Others might call it a predictable, psychological by-product of having been uprooted from one culture and taken to another, then deserted by her father who left his transplanted family and returned to Sicily after finding he could not adjust to this new, unfathomable place.

But my guess is that her melancholy stemmed from the trauma of having her language taken away almost immediately upon stepping foot on U.S. soil. She was the youngest of thirteen children and, with her mother, was the last of the Giacalones to join the family in Louisville. To become an American in those days was to melt into the pot, as butter does in water set to boiling. Part of the process was to shed the outer trappings of Old World language, dress, and custom, as a clove of garlic must give up its skin to become part of the soup.

In my grandmother's case, there was nothing slow or gradual about the melting-pot process. Her older brothers, by then well versed in the facts of immigrant life, urged their mother to teach Victoria to speak English as quickly as possible. They suggested she stay for a while at a Catholic orphanage not far from where they lived. There she would have no reason to speak Italian and every opportunity to master English.

Her mother complied. Victoria once told me she did not live at the orphanage long—but long enough. When she returned to her family, she could speak "American" without a trace of her native tongue creeping in and giving her away. There was but one problem: She could no longer speak Italian. She could not understand her mother's long-anticipated words welcoming her home. Nor could her mother comprehend the curious jumble of unfamiliar sounds that tumbled from her daughter's mouth as the two embraced.

Eventually my grandmother came up with a compromise language, an improvised pidgin-Italian I often heard her use with her cousins later in life. Like her steaming dishes of pasta, this odd patois was most evident at holidays or on other occasions when emotions ran high. Funerals. Births. First Communions. It was a hodgepodge tongue she fashioned—a pinch of Italian sprinkled here and there, spicing up an otherwise-bland English sentence.

Once, long ago, my grandmother spoke and was not understood. I can imagine her deciding, perhaps as a young woman, that this would not happen again. There would be meatballs and pasta on the table, always. There would be bowls of freshly grated cheese, not green cardboard shakers of tasteless yellow powder. Her food would speak of a life and land, and we, her disinclined descendants, would be forced to listen.

Mom's Potato Dumplings

eight medium russet potatoes with their jackets on (do not use baking
    potatoes)
one egg, lightly beaten
one onion, cut in four or five pieces
two slices stale bread
two tablespoons flour
two teaspoons salt
gravy, optional

Bring potatoes to a boil in a pot of water. Do not overcook. They should be still firm in the middle. Set aside to cool. Remove the skins of the potatoes, and use a Foley mill or ricer to grind. Add the hard bread and onion, a little at a time, while grinding. Add the egg to the potato mixture. Blend all ingredients with some flour. Stir to a firm but flexible consistency by hand. Do not over-stir to a "too-tight" mixture. Bring a large pot of salted water to a boil. Prepare a large breadboard by covering it with one layer of waxed paper. Flour the paper lightly. Shape the mixture into balls about the size of a medium lemon. While forming the dumplings, keep your hands lightly floured to prevent sticking. Adjust the boiling water to a very gentle boil. Using a large spoon, gently ladle the dumplings into the water—about six at a time. Do not crowd. Dumplings will rise rapidly to the top when ready. Remove quickly and place in a bowl. Ladle with gravy. Serves six.

The heart of any home is its kitchen. I learned this at an impressionable age, not in my mother's house but during weekends spent at *her* mother's house. At home, my mother ruled over a one-woman kitchen, a cramped little room where two people constituted a crowd. Other than a few simple dishes, she did not teach me to cook. She said there was no room for anyone else in that square patch of workspace. Her kitchen was her domain, whatever its shortcomings. Though she complained of never having the right utensils or pots or dishes, she made do.

At my grandmother's house, a stone cottage on a wide avenue in a city neighborhood known as the Highlands, there was always plenty of everything. I lived miles away in the suburbs, in a post-war subdivision with front yards that ended in drainage ditches that merged with the blacktop of our road, and with backyards that ran smack up against the yards of the houses on the street behind us. But my grandmother's backyard bordered a brick alley and had a patterned sidewalk in front. The treetops met in the middle of the road, forming a tunnel of leaves most of the year, a canopy of oaks and maples that made me feel connected to something old and established.

As did the cooking that went on in that kitchen. It was plentiful, yes, but more than that it was a process. And I was a part of it. No food from cans or boxes for *my* grandmother, who was called Mom by everyone in the family. Under Mom's patient guidance, I learned to prepare vegetables and sift flour, scrape carrots and peel potatoes—efficiently and creatively. With a kitchen knife, Mom taught me to shave a single unbroken spiral of skin from the top of a potato to its bottom. Work became a game; peeling potatoes, an art.

Potatoes, in fact, were the staple of my grandmother's household. We ate them boiled, fried, mashed, roasted, sliced, diced, riced and—to my delight—raw. Nothing to me in those days was quite so sweet or exotic as a freshly cut chunk of peeled, uncooked potato, creamy white and succulent with a crunch to each bite. We ate hash browns, and we ate potato pancakes—my grandmother with her shiny spatula slapping them hot off the griddle onto our plates.

On special occasions, when the karma was right and my grandmother was up to the task, we ate potato dumplings. They were her nod to both the German and the Irish in her background. They were part myth, much mystery: the pièce de résistance of her never-idle kitchen. If Victoria's meatballs forced themselves upon us, Mom's dumplings seduced us. The name itself sounds like a term of endearment lovers might use.

Potato dumplings, to me, are the essence of comfort food: hot, soft, white, and miraculously healing of whatever it is that ails you. Chicken soup now has the endorsement of scientists who have identified its elixir-like properties. Potato dumplings still must be accepted on faith. Blessed are those who eat steamed, simmering balls of chopped potatoes, for they shall inherit the recipe.

Here is how I remember the ritual of making potato dumplings:

Take several women related by blood. Dress them in aprons. Give them mugs of hot coffee. Start them working early in the morning, perhaps even the day before. Let them argue about the finer points of the recipe. This is the spice that is needed.

Watch them peel, chop, add, mix, rice, roll, taste, set aside, submerge, pray, leave the room, wring their hands, return to watch the pot, sigh, curse, cry, beseech others to pray . . .

The women perform their ritual always with the dark knowledge that, in the end, the potatoes must make a choice. They can rise to the top of the steaming pot, round white clouds of luscious perfection adrift on a simmering sea. Or they can fall apart, or sink to the bottom of the pot, heavy lumps of unfulfilled potato dough, consigned to an underworld of failure and defeat. My aunt Aileen, who succeeded my grandmother as the keeper of the recipe, remembers only one occasion when the dumplings disappointed, but there must have been more. Why else the anxiety? The wringing of hands? The fussing over the pot?

My mother's last Thanksgiving took place, for the most part, in her mother's kitchen. By then, Mom was dead, and my aunt Aileen occupied the house. I have hung on to two photographs snapped that day. One shows my mother by the dumpling pot on the old Chambers stove, her hands on her hips, her reading glasses low on her nose, her eyes boring into the lens as if to say to me, hidden behind the camera: "I've got to get back to these potatoes. Hurry up!" The other photograph is a close-up: rows and rows of potato balls lined up on a floured bread board, awaiting their turn to be tested.

How odd, I think sometimes when I happen upon that snapshot in the drawer where I keep it. How truly odd that for both sides of my family, the shape of comfort is a ball. Recently it struck me that it is the same for Josh, who loves matzo ball soup not so much for its rich, soothing broth but for the golden orbs within it that give texture and dimension. This is the shape of the love that encircles us, of the lost worlds that persist, of memories that can be counted upon to rise to the surface, unpredictably, miraculously, against all odds, even when we think we have forgotten them.

∽Dianne Aprile is a writer for the *Courier-Journal*. Her Sunday columns earned first-place awards from The National Society of Newspaper Columnists and the Society of Professional Journalists. She received an Al Smith Fellowship from the Kentucky Arts Council and a Kentucky Foundation for Women grant for fiction writing. She teaches creative writing in Bellarmine's continuing education program. A collection of her personal essays, *The Things We Don't Forget: Views from Real Life*, is in its second printing (Trout Lily Press, 1996) and has been adapted for stage. She is currently writing a book on the Abbey of Gethsemani, home of the writer Thomas Merton and the oldest Trappist monastery in America. Her work has appeared in *Kentucky Voices: A Bicentennial Celebration of Writing and The Dark Woods I Cross: An Anthology of Contemporary Louisville Women Poets*. She lives in Louisville with her husband and son.

Sunday's Legacies

L. Elisabeth Beattie

When I think of family my meaning extends to encompass the living and the dead, the latter rendered real for me by the ancestral antiques and tales of their owners I memorized as a child in the crook of my grandmother's arm. Sunday-go-to-meeting day—as Grandmother Watts still called Sundays even in the 1950s—meant, in the dazzling heat of St. Charles, Missouri, nestling next to her in church and folding fans from the lily-bordered bulletins I'd extract from the plastic pockets nailed to the back of the pew; meant hearing hymns ancient and plaintive and slightly off-key rise and fall to the rhythms of the bulletins' easy snap and sway; and meant seeking in the arched and brilliant stained glass windows stories more vivid, even, than the colorful sermons.

Then Sundays called for heading home—sometimes to our house, the white wooden ranch on West Adams Street with its exploding purple clematis vines where with me my parents, my brother, and my pet-of-the-moment lived—but more often to Grandmother's crosstown bungalow to play beneath her front lawn's lacy mimosas as she tied on her apron and prepared in what seemed minutes a feast disguised as a meal.

As I devised from the dwelling's wrought-iron-rail-lined concrete steps and flowering bushes a schoolhouse framed by a blue hydrangea door, a portal my almost-four-years-younger brother could trespass only at the fickle discretion of my school-marmy will—Grandmother floured the chicken she afterwards fried to crisp, crust-flecked perfection.

While Mom set the table with the same Blue Willow china and Depression glass tumblers that had served her and her brother in their youth, and while Dad perused the heftiest newspaper of the week—the *St. Louis Post-Dispatch* that harbored among its plethora of inky treasures crossword puzzles and the comic adventures of Pogo—Grandmother turned out corn pudding; high-risen biscuits rolled from scratch; string beans steeped in salted butter; and rich, flaky pie—always pie. Sometimes the latticed dessert that bubbled and oozed as Grandmother delivered it, piping hot, to the embroidered-clothed table, trickled—translucent and red—onto the cross-stitched chrysanthemums. If the juice ran pale gold onto the cloth, or if graham cracker crumbs rained atop the Xed flowers and birds that Grandmother had needled into being, I'd know the pie wasn't cherry that Sunday, but peach from the trees in our own backyard, or lemonade—a concoction whose casual instructions (a dollop of this, a speck of that) appeared scratched in indigo ink on a brittle, brown-edged notecard tucked in the metal recipe file long-before presented to Grandmother as a going away gift from a still-thriving out-of-town chapter of the stalwart DAR.

Then, as now, as my silhouette will attest, dessert constituted my favorite course at any meal, breakfast included, if I could substitute cinnamon-swirled coffee cake for the usual no-nonsense bowl of cold, Quaker-plain cereal. And Grandmother's pies—the recipes and culinary skill which my mother inherited—and promises, should I ever linger in a kitchen long enough to prepare as well as to partake of an entire meal, she'll pass on to me—made the sweetest conclusions to Sunday afternoons.

After dinner, while Grandmother and Mom washed the dishes—all the while exchanging the gossip referred to in that still-genteel era as "news"—and while Dad worked the crosswords as my brother, still a toddler, toppled over toys at Dad's feet, I held court at the dining room table, Grandmother's rose-splashed Victorian chocolate pot and her prized collection of porcelain cups and saucers having been brought to me from their shrine, the glass-encased china cabinet, and entrusted to my care. For me, each gilded, hand-painted cup and saucer held lives and stories I could fathom if I focused on the bow-tied garlands or the golden legs or the fluted lips that distinguished each demitasse profile. In the midst of fancying myself the doyenne of a duchy more exotic than my Midwestern lot allowed, Grandmother would slip back to the table, her domestic tasks finished or at least set aside, take me in her arms, and transport me with her family stories to the days of her girlhood and to her ancestors' youths.

My stomach satiated with pie and hot chocolate, my head filled with images of the long-ago capers of my forebears who emigrated first from England to Virginia, then from Virginia to Kentucky, to land in Missouri for what would be more than a century, I lolled in Grandmother's ample lap—my mind and my heart in sleepy, subconscious collusion—coupling family with sustenance and sustenance with stories. For me, curled as I was in Grandmother's lap, pulling her ear while sneaking comforting, clandestine sucks on my six-year-old thumb, stories explored life's essence.

My childhood Sundays served not as the beginning or end of every week, but as the nucleus from which all other days sprang. The parables Grandmother couched as memories, seasoned by the casual ceremonies of ritual meals, incarnated for me the vital significance of tolerance and strength, as well as the importance of integrity gained through nurturing others, family members and strangers alike.

Now living with me and my father and my assemblage of rescued cats in Louisville, Kentucky, in the late 1990s, my mother is the age my grandmother was more than thirty years ago when, with the virtuoso panache of an aproned maestro, she orchestrated our unparalleled Sunday meals. Here at the cusp of the millennium, my mother, too, concocts tawny baked chicken, tasty corn, and seasoned beans, but in this health-concious era she eliminates evil fats and cholesterol from the rich, caloric dishes of our childhoods. And desserts, of course—even on Sundays—have come to constitute in our science-minded, anorexia-prone culture-of-perfection—as well as in Mom's contemporary kitchen—almost a moral taboo. So the pies Mom mixes from Grandmother's recipe cards she now bakes guilt-free only for holidays or for company meals, occasions when food in its unabashed excess still serves as a metaphor for emotional, not just physical, love.

Even as our habits have changed, age and commitments too many to count have altered our family, rendering lazy Sundays rare. Over the decades my circle of relatives has broken and spread across states; time between reunions now stretches, substituting hurried, annual meetings for the languorous, weekly encounters of old.

Yet at Thanksgiving and Christmas crispy bits of buttered fowl and honey-coated pie crumbs still sprinkle the same cross-stitched tablecloth that served my parents at mid-century, and that served their parents in 1900, when the promise of pioneering a new era must have loomed infinite, large.

Today, Mom, good a cook as she is, prefers mixing acrylics on canvas to combining ingredients atop a hot stove. I, too, can cook a bit—can bake the basic cakes and pies I tote to civic potlucks. But like Mom, my primary passion took a different turn. I'd rather spend Sunday afternoons teasing ideas into words than kneading dough, as my hunger for immersing myself in the smooth flow of prose is every bit as intense and as necessary to my health as is my need for daily bread. Yet both Mom and I know that no matter whether we dwell in our kitchens, reside in other regions, or linger in the realms of our arts, the recipes that nourished our childhoods—like our memories of their makers—will continue to feed our souls.

Grandmother's Basic Pie Crust

crust for a nine-inch, lattice-top pie:
three-fourths cup solid shortening, such as Crisco
one-fourth cup boiling water
one tablespoon milk
two cups sifted flour
one teaspoon salt

Put shortening in a mixing bowl. Add boiling water and milk; with a fork, break up shortening. Tilt bowl, and with rapid strokes whip until mixture is smooth and thick like whipped cream. Sift flour and salt together into shortening mixture. Stir quickly, pick up, and knead into smooth dough. After moistening a counter surface with a damp cloth, cover the counter space with waxed paper. Place one-half of the dough on the paper, and cover the dough with more waxed paper. Roll out dough so it extends beyond the size of the pie pan. Remove one layer of waxed paper and place dough in pie pan.

Remove second layer of waxed paper. Take remaining dough and, between waxed paper, roll thin and flat. Then, with a knife, cut into even, half-inch strips. After preparing pie filling and before baking, drape strips vertically, then horizontally, over the filling.

Grandmother's Cherry Pie Filling

In a saucepan, mix together three-fourths to one cup sugar, four tablespoons flour, and one-fourth teaspoon almond extract, as well as one-fourth teaspoon cinnamon, if desired. Stir in two and one-half cups sour red pie cherries and juice. Cook over moderate heat, stirring constantly, until mixture boils and thickens. Pour into pastry-lined pie pan. Cover filling with latticed dough strips. Dot between latticed dough with one and one-third tablespoons butter. Bake in preheated, 425 degree oven for thirty to forty minutes.

Grandmother's Fresh Peach Pie

In a nine-inch, unbaked pie shell, arrange four cups of fresh, peeled peaches cut into one-fourth-inch slices. In a mixing bowl, combine one to one and one-fourth cups sugar, three tablespoons flour, and a dash of salt. Pour sugar mixture over peaches. Add latticed pie strips, then dot exposed peach mixture with butter. Bake until brown, approximately thirty to forty minutes, in a preheated, 425 degree oven.

Grandmother's Graham Cracker Pie Crust (for a nine-inch single crust)

Crush with a rolling pin one and one-half cups graham cracker crumbs. Stir into the crumbs until well blended, one-fourth to one-half cup confectioners' sugar, six tablespoons melted butter, and one teaspoon cinnamon. Pat into the pan. Bake at 350 degrees for eight minutes, and cool the empty shell before filling.

Grandmother's Lemonade Pie Filling

In a large mixing bowl, fold together one six-ounce can of frozen lemonade that has been thawed to room temperature, one fourteen-ounce can of condensed milk, and one cup of whipped cream (made from whipping heavy cream into stiff peaks, then blending in two teaspoons sugar). Fold together, then add the juice and grated rind of one lemon. Pour into a nine-inch graham cracker crust and freeze.

∾L. (Linda) Elisabeth Beattie, born in Wisconsin and raised in Missouri and upstate New York, earned her Ed.D. in Leadership Education from Spalding University; her M.A.T. in English from the University of Louisville; her M.A. in Magazine Journalism from Syracuse University's Newhouse School of Public Communication; and her B.A. in English Literature, English Composition, and Oral History from Beloit College. A ten-year Louisvillian employed for eight years as an associate professor of English and Journalism at Elizabethtown Community College, Beattie balances teaching with writing, a career that has included publishing essays, criticism, and feature articles in more than 700 regional and national newspapers and magazines. In 1996, the University Press of Kentucky published Beattie's book, *Conversations With Kentucky Writers*, and plans to publish her forthcoming sequel. A recipient of grants from the Kentucky Oral History Commission and the Kentucky Foundation for Women, Beattie spends her out-of-classroom time researching and writing books, reading for pleasure, and coddling her coterie of refugee cats.

The Proof of Mother's Puddings

JOY BALE BOONE

As a child, my Christmas began in autumn. Though the event was temporarily forgotten by me when birthdays, Halloween, and Thanksgiving came along, its sweet solemnity was renewed when a plum pudding, top ablaze, each year made triumphant entrance into my parents' dining room on December 25.

I was three or four years of age when first allowed to watch the plum pudding ritual. In those days, children started school with kindergarten, not day care, so it didn't matter which day Mother chose to devote to her one culinary distinction, provided, of course, that it wasn't her weekly day of leisure when friends came to call.

After I entered the primary grades, plum pudding day always fell on Saturdays. Only when I was older did I realize Mother had accommodated me. When I grew from childhood into my teens, my interest became more outward and lively, and I eventually forsook Mother's day of shared magic. But my guilt is retroactive. I have come to treasure the thought that for nearly ten years I owned Mother's undivided attention for at least one day each annum. I felt honored to stir, bake, and sample in the kitchen with mother with time out for lunch, for a languorous nap during the early years, and for seemingly endless sips of aromatic afternoon tea.

Other than on those precious plum pudding days, I seldom saw Mother in our kitchen except when she passed through it to head for the garage, and on to market or to pay a social visit or to pick up a child from school. On Sundays she would hustle directly from the Episcopal church to give the last-minute touch to the Yorkshire pudding our cook had started. My parents, who came to the States as bride and groom from England, never lost their accents, their traditions, or their bland Yorkshire puddings. Yet Mother entrusted puddings of the Yorkshire variety to take shape in another's hands. Mother reserved *her* kitchen presence for the concoction and care of her singular culinary masterpiece, her savory plum pudding.

Mother never encouraged culinary questions. Together in the kitchen, she and I, we were mostly quiet, speaking—if at all—in whispers. I watched Mother cut pale green citron in ever-smaller pieces. I stood by her side as she carved crystallized orange and lemon peels into sparkling shapes that struck me as a magical, aromatic melding of shapes and colors smooth and glorious as stained glass. And I can never forget the exotic smells of the mace, nutmeg, and cinnamon Mother blended into the heady mix. Such sights and scents transported me to reveries of Wise Men's myrrh. As Mother labored intently, I saw turbans and casks of gold.

Sound, too, accompanied our solemn plum pudding ritual. Brinky, our brindle bull terrier, snored softly in his basket at the foot of the back stairs. Perhaps he dreamed of sugarplums, those fruits Canadians call saskatoons. Now, as then, it came as a comfort to know that sugarplum trees are more than mere fantasies. The yellow canary in the adjoining room sang joyously, accompanying Brinky's canine snore, causing Mother's performance to rise to the pinnacle of full orchestration.

After Mother had enriched the pudding's smooth dough with candied fruits, spices, and other delights, she forced the mixture into molds resembling miniature replicas of pyramids I'd seen in full-color, Sunday school renditions of *The Book of Knowledge*. By then the water-filled kettles awaited the rich concoction. After Mother steamed the puddings for six hours, she—with help from our maid—cautiously removed them from the stove, while I observed the rite from a respectful distance. Then Mother unwrapped the puddings—usually three or four in number—and gently wrapped them in the flannel cloths I regarded as swaddling clothes. Snug in their warm, brandy-soaked flannel that complemented the sherry with which my otherwise-teetotaling mother had sprinkled the dough, the puddings then rested three months or so in the chocolate-colored crocks that lined our pantry shelves.

My good-natured father stayed away from the kitchen during plum pudding days. He could rarely resist a witticism or a slapstick joke, much less a pun, and even on an ordinary day, Mother frowned when he laughed too long at his jokes. He took no offense but, slapping his thigh, he'd often exclaim, "Good Lord, Edie, if I didn't think it was funny, I wouldn't have said it." Mother's sacred day in the kitchen was neither the place nor the time for levity.

Despite my loss of interest in pudding preparations during my teen years, I retained unrestrained enthusiasm for the Christmas teas to which Auntie Lil, an English friend of the family's, took my mother, my older sister, and me each yuletide season. After a few years, my younger sister, too, was old enough to be added to the favored guest list. The setting was the Fountain Room at Marshall Field's. The approach to the elevators that ascended to the tea room revealed a dazzlement of Christmas. An enormous Christmas tree reaching up, up past many floors to the top of the nearly sky-high atrium overwhelmed me, but my greatest excitement was the large, round oranges that Auntie Lil had brought from her greengrocer and placed by our plates that rested on the dining room table's thick damask cloth. How sweet the oranges smelled even before they reached our hands. The pretty waitresses in black with white ruffled aprons brought extraordinary bell-, wreath-, and holly-shaped sweets to our table, yet such fragile and sugarspun delicacies failed to surpass Lil's succulent extravagances.

Usually, a large orange appeared in each of our Christmas stockings, too, tempting us as they rounded out the stockings' woolen toes. Our stockings never hung by the chimney with care; instead they drooped, suspended from the crooks of our bedposts, an advantage that allowed us to explore their riches in the privacy of our rooms when we awakened Christmas morning—a privacy, I recall, that lent a special thrill, as if Santa might still lurk nearby. After the glee of small gifts, the orange appeared. I always peeled mine, permitting the pungent juice to trickle down my chin.

Later, my family joined together to open our big gifts we retrieved from beside the crackling fire and from under the tree, yet even those did not quite compare with my own private Christmas upstairs. Mother exhibited great interest in each gift, as if she'd never seen it before, while Father sang, his marvelous voice accompanying the carols on the phonograph. Frequently, Father punctuated his music with laughter. He, too, had his private pleasures.

By early afternoon, turkey, stuffing (scooped with our long-handled silver serving spoon), cranberry sauce, a cornucopia of vegetables and salads, and colorful non-food crackers dressed our dining room table. In England an edible cracker is called a biscuit. A celebratory cracker, a party cracker, is a light cardboard tube covered in colorful paper. When I was young, the covering consisted of red or green crinkly crepe with tinsel of some sort for glitter. A narrow tape with a tiny explosive device at its middle runs through a cracker's tube. We pulled each end of our crackers' tapes so that as they popped and banged they split apart, divulging favors, fortunes, and paper hats. We partied merrily, we heads with paper crowns!

After the food and fun came the pudding carried into the dining room, flames licking the holly sprig perched high atop the lofty dessert. Not even my father found cause for wit as my mother gravely sliced her *pièce de résistance*. As Mother passed slices around the table, she and I always shared a smile. The spirits that had danced around the pudding's crown as a holiday communion gave way as we drove our sterling spoons into the pudding's dense core, in search of a hidden token. A ring, a charm for a watch chain, a small glass flower, whatever trinket mother had buried, was meant to hasten good fortune in the lucky recipient's new year. However I, like my siblings, took heart—were we not the token's finders—in the fact that luck could also be captured and consumed by downing a spoonful of pudding still lit by a flickering flame.

Through my adult years there have been plenty of wisecracks about "The Cooking of Joy." Perhaps because as a young wife and mother I set weekly dinner menus of foods most of the children at one sitting would eat, I wasn't considered imaginative enough to attain a chef rating. Roast beef hash on Mondays, pork chops on Tuesdays, meat loaf the next day, chili or something like that on Thursdays, a simple fish on Fridays (in deference to my parents' religious ways), steaks or lamb chops on Saturdays, and always roast beef on Sundays. Each of my children knew which nights to inveigle dinner invitations from friends. I didn't have a cook as Mother had, so my time for preparing dinner always arrived after my general practitioner husband closed his office to make house calls. My cooking time also coincided with my children's homework questions and frequent phone calls from my husband's patients.

Even recognizing that my background for confident *cordon bleu* has been limited over the years, friends and family alike, with few exceptions, have enjoyed repeating the many stories of my cooking *contretemps*. Aside from my oldest child, Shelby, telling his five siblings that I was the fastest cook they'd ever see, my culinary talents have been somewhat maligned. My son told his brothers and sisters that one evening he had timed my cooking for nine (a neighbor's child dropped in to add to our family's nuclear number). I had prepared a dozen pork chops, French fries, peas, and opened a jar of applesauce while answering the telephone seven times, jotting down patients' messages, breaking up a heated battle, and yelling for someone please to answer the children's telephone upstairs. Shelby testified that, for all the commotion, our meal was ready in thirty-one minutes.

Actually, I've had only two real cooking disasters in my life, not counting the time I tried to bring past and present together. I bought a plum pudding from a highly recommended maker of such up the road. Residing, by that time, in the Bible Belt, I knew Mrs. McNamara's pudding wouldn't possess the flair of my mother's, but I hoped a purloined bottle of brandy would assure a flame. I made sure I had holly, too. The place was my mother-in-law's home, the occasion Christmas dinner. I had been granted privilege of kitchen to prepare my much-anticipated dessert. I chose to take sole charge of the proceedings, so the flaming pudding would surprise everyone as I carried it into the dining room.

Everything was ready, brandy at hand, matchbox beside it, pudding firmly on the plate. With care to pour over the pudding the precise amount of brandy to fuel the flames, I touched a match to the liquid. Nothing happened. I poured more brandy, again struck a match, and again nothing happened. By then, shaking, I managed a third and final futile try, the smell of spirits having all the while increased. Giving up at last, I marched the pudding to the festive table, where, despite paper hats cocked jauntily on heads, even the holly appeared crestfallen. Much later I discovered that the blue-orange flames of the brandy had leapt after all, and probably at the touch of my first match. But their glow had not shown under the flourescent lights of my mother-in-law's modern kitchen.

A much earlier culinary tale of woe came to hurt even worse. I had been married only a few weeks, temporarily living in the New York apartment of two professors who were in Europe on sabbatical. Broke to a penny on a daily basis, not yet able to find a job, I was thrilled when I received the then-handsome sum of a five-dollar check as a gift. The era was the Depression, and since my young husband, as an intern, had to remain on hospital duty two nights out of three, I decided to provide him a real dinner on his next night at home.

From my palmier days, I knew the kind of dinners men liked. Walking to market feeling like a well-to-do housewife, I bought two T-bone steaks, a few potatoes, and a can of Crisco shortening. I also bought peas in their pods, and two ears of corn. Since I couldn't purchase just two, I skipped buying rolls. They would have called for butter, anyway. I don't think I thought of dessert, for who eats plum pudding in hot weather? My thoughtlessness didn't matter, though, for as things turned out, *dessert* would have been a misnomer.

I walked home, a happy woman, carrying groceries in all my glory. I stayed happy as I sculpted round potatoes into curved slices. My despondency started when I watched the heated Crisco evaporate into almost none. I'd had no idea that its solid state would diminish in the bottoms of my pans atop the stove. Then my peas disappeared, the contents of green pods also revealing the deceit of their inflated disguise. Two or three lone peas fell from the pods that appeared ready to burst. I took comfort in the fact that at least the two ears of corn seemed ripe and full. But as I ate a niblet or two, my mood darkened. I dropped the cobs in boiling water. Then I put the steaks in the oven too soon, baking them before I remembered having heard about broiling.

When my husband arrived for his surprise, he found me in tears. Even worse, he found me in pain. The raw corn I'd consumed had caused terrible stomach cramps, a condition my doctor husband soon diagnosed. Years later, my husband confessed that as he ate them, he had counted all the peas I'd prepared: fifteen. We hadn't divided them by two. After all, I was sick.

When the professors returned to their apartment overlooking the

Hudson, I necessarily moved farther into town to a fifth-floor, single-room walk-up where I shared a bathroom with five strangers. Having only a hot plate and a small Sterno outfit for making tea, there were no occasions for dinners, and my husband took all his meals at the hospital. Wives were allowed to come for free, Sunday-noon dinners, a privilege well worth walking the seventeen New York blocks past the Church of Heavenly Rest.

Almost a decade later, after my husband and I had moved to Kentucky after World War II, I experienced a rare surge of domesticity one sunny afternoon, a feeling I gave way to by baking a lemon pie. The pie coalesced in the oven while I mixed the ingredients for meringue. Much later a friend told me that the poorly written recipe assumed too much, but reading to the best of my analytical ability, I arranged the meringue mixture in a saucepan on top of the stove.

Another disappearing act. Poof! I ingeniously decided to make another mix of egg whites, and instead of cooking it separately, I poured the meringue atop the pie baking in the oven. My notion worked beautifully, and bursting with pride in my newly found cooking sense, I rushed to the telephone to tell my mother-in-law—the seasoned and splendid cook whose lemon pies I'd enjoyed for quite some years—I'd created a better way to cover pies with meringue. But my kind, loving, and supportive mother-in-law seemed to be stifling laughter. That success I should have kept to myself I confided to several friends. Hence, the story traveled.

Studies have shown that taste buds change as one matures, and that often what tasted extra good as one's mother cooked it does not taste the same in one's later years. True or false, my daughters-in-law never have had to listen to those discouraging words about wishing they could cook like Mother. It may be why they and I get along so well. My own two daughters are fine cooks, and so is one son. The other sons married good cooks, so they specialize in things like pancakes with pure maple syrup, steaks broiled over a charcoal grill, and popcorn.

When my mother gentled into advanced age, she spent a few years with my husband, me, and the two children still living at home. She was happy in the presence of books, and though I would frequently find her reading one upside down, I knew she felt content simply from cradling bound pages in her hands. Usually, when she closed a volume at any age, she'd say with satisfaction, "Well, I've finished THAT one!" Of course. There's more than one way to finish a book.

One quiet evening as we sat in the library together, I asked Mother if she ever thought about the brandied puddings in their sealed brown crocks in the pantries of our two long-ago homes. For a moment she looked at me very hard. I was afraid I'd offended some delicate balance deep within her. But then her face softened. She smiled. I had my answer. And I hoped her memory proved as fulfilling as mine.

English Plum Pudding

one cup all-purpose flour
one teaspoon baking soda
one teaspoon salt
one teaspoon cinnamon
three-fourths teaspoon mace
one-fourth teaspoon nutmeg
one and one-half cups chopped raisins
two cups currants
three-fourths cup finely cut citron
one-third cup candied orange peel
one-third cup candied lemon peel
one-half cup finely chopped walnuts
one and one-half cups bread crumbs
two cups ground suet
one cup brown sugar, packed
three eggs, beaten
one-third cup currant jelly
one-fourth cup orange juice

Grease a two-quart ring mold. Measure flour, soda, salt, cinnamon, mace, and nutmeg into a large bowl. Stir in fruits, nuts, and bread crumbs. Mix suet, brown sugar, eggs, jelly, and fruit juice, and stir into flour-fruit mixture. Pour into mold. Cover mold with aluminum foil.

Place rack in Dutch oven and pour boiling water into pan up to level of rack. Place filled mold on rack. Cover Dutch oven. Keep water boiling over low heat to steam pudding approximately four hours.

Turn pudding out of mold, cut into slices, and serve warm with Hard Sauce. Yield: Sixteen servings

Hard Sauce

one-half cup butter or margarine, softened
one cup confectioners' sugar
two teaspoons vanilla

Mix together all ingredients. Chill at least one hour. For a flaming pudding, pour heated brandy on pudding and light with a match.

∿Born in 1912 in Chicago, Illinois, Joy Field, Kentucky's current poet laureate, moved at age six to Evanston, Illinois, where she lived—with time out for newspaper work in Miami Beach, Florida, and at the *Chicago Daily News*—before her 1934 marriage to Kentuckian Garnett Bale. After his medical internship in New York City, his residency in Louisville, and a year living in Lynch, Kentucky, the Bales settled in Elizabethtown, Kentucky, where they raised their six children. Three years after her husband's death in 1972, she married George Street Boone and moved to his Elkton, Kentucky, home. Boone, who now resides in Elkton and Glasgow, Kentucky, served as founder and editor of the statewide literary magazine *Approaches*, that later became *The Kentucky Poetry Review*, and since its inception has chaired the Center for Robert Penn Warren Studies at Western Kentucky University. For more than fifty years Boone has reviewed books for local and regional newspapers, has served on the Board of Directors of the Thomas Clark Foundation for the University Press of Kentucky, and has published three books, *Never Less Than Love*, *The Storm's Eye*, and *Even Without Love*. In addition to her literary pursuits, Boone is a past state president of the League of Women Voters, the Friends of Kentucky Libraries, and the Kentucky Mental Health Association. Recognition of Boone's contributions to Kentucky include her designation by Kentucky Educational Television as a Distinguished Kentuckian and her selection by the University of Kentucky as a winner of the Sullivan Award.

My Sister, the Rabbit, and the Roll

Marie Bradby

Until recently, anytime that I visited my parents, my mother would make rolls. It was a reward for driving eleven hours. But my parents are getting up in years. During my last visits, I did all the cooking. For Thanksgiving, my mother even resorted to frozen rolls. I watched her slit open the plastic package and arrange the pale balls of frozen dough in a pan. She leaned against the counter for support. It pained me to watch. As I drove home, my mind slipped back to my earliest memory of bread baking. It was a day with a curious beginning.

It was summer, and I was three years old. I ran from room to room playing with my older brothers and sister. On one trip through my parents' bedroom, my father scooped me up in his arms and hugged me. "I'm going out for a little bit," he said, "but when I come back, I'm going to bring you the prettiest little rabbit you ever saw." I had goose bumps all over. It was the happiest moment of my life. He set me down and gathered up things from the bureau and put them in a small beige suitcase that had a pearl handle. He even picked up a few things from my old crib. I didn't sleep there any more. My mother used it to store folded clothes.

I ran off and didn't even notice when my father left. My grandmother was making rolls. From the moment I would hear the scrape of the sifter as she turned the handle, my mouth would water for one of those soft, buttery brown pillows of bread. Beside the rolls, I loved being near my grandmother even though she didn't pay much attention to me. But it's hard to get much attention in a house full of six children, even if you are the baby.

My father returned. My mother was with him. She had been away for several days, though I wasn't sure why. He helped my mother upstairs to their bedroom. The older children helped, too. I was supposed to stay downstairs with my aunt, who had arrived with her two small boys. But I snuck upstairs in no time, crawled onto my mother's lap, and laid my head on her breasts. She smelled like milk. We cuddled for a minute until I remembered my father's promise. He was rummaging around in the crib. I went up to him and pulled on his pant leg. "Where's the rabbit?" I asked.

"Rabbit?" he said, as if I was speaking another language.

"Did you bring the rabbit?" I asked.

"Oh, let me show you what we've got here," he said, and lifted me up and held me over the crib. "This is your new sister. She's the prettiest little baby in the whole wide world." I was unimpressed. I had never really seen a baby before. This one wore a pink gown and had a head full of large black ringlets. She was sound asleep. What did you do with babies? I wondered. Why, *I* was the baby. We didn't need another one.

I reached out to touch the baby, her lips perfectly pulled into a bow, her fist clutching my father's finger. My father guided my hand to pat her gently on her side. She looked like one of my sister's dolls. Then I looked at him as I hung suspended in disbelief over the crib, "But where's the rabbit?" He put me down.

"There isn't any rabbit. I meant that I was bringing you a new little sister," he said, as if that was supposed to be special. But I didn't get it.

My father is a gentle person. I had taken his words literally. I didn't know that adults don't always mean what they say. I cried. He tried to comfort me as I flopped up and down on the floor. My mother shushed me, telling me not to wake the baby. My aunt finally rushed into the room and took me downstairs. The older children were setting the dining room table. My grandmother and my aunt—both slim, hard-working women—were cooking. I could hear them clanging pots and stirring sizzling food. I curled up in a big armchair in the corner of the dining room and stewed, my shoulders heaving and my nose running.

As I whined, I watched my brothers put all the leaves in the dining room table until it nearly filled the room along with the smells from the kitchen: fried chicken, fried croakers, fried potatoes, fried apples, sausage, shad roe cakes, scrambled eggs, bacon, and the sweet smell of bread baking. Yes! That meant rolls with lots and lots of butter. I'd seen my grandmother make them many times. She would mix the sticky dough with her brown knarled fingers and scrape it back into the bowl. She would knead the dough on the kitchen table, slapping it and pounding it. The result would be a pan of golden brown rolls that she would pull out of the oven and butter the tops. Eating one was just as good as eating ice cream.

I didn't have to be called twice to the table that Sunday morning. I quit my fussing and knelt on the chair that I had to share with my brother. My grandmother said the blessing. She leaned her forehead on her folded hands and prayed and prayed. When Grandma was done, the food was passed around. I kept my eyes on the rolls.

As someone was buttering one for me, there was a knock at the door. Reverend Mills, our pastor, had come to visit. "Well, I see I'm just in time," he said, hat in hand. He was offered a seat at the table that someone had to get out of. He took off his black suit coat, hung it on the back of the chair, and sat down. After inquiring about my mother and the "new baby," he prayed. He stood up and held out his arms and called for all the good blessings to come into our home. This took a very long time. I kept my eyes open and watched my roll. My aunt had it. When Reverend Mills finished, he announced, "I just love your rolls, Mrs. Adams." My grandmother blushed and grabbed the basket. It was empty. Everyone who had not already shoved his roll into his mouth guarded what was on his plate.

"Oh!" my aunt began, "I believe this is the last roll, Reverend," she said sweetly, holding out her hand.

"That's my roll!" I said.

"Oh, little girl, I hope you don't mind if I take your roll," he said, reaching for it. "I'm sure you've already had some earlier."

"No, I didn't," I said.

"But you get to eat your grandmother's rolls all the time," he said.

"It's all right," my grandmother said, being polite, "I'll make some more rolls."

Reverend Mills didn't waste another second. He took the honey-colored roll and shoved it halfway into his mouth. I wailed. "But that's my roll!" My aunt tried to console me, saying this and that and picking me up and walking around with me. But no one offered to give me his roll. My grandmother looked goo-goo-eyed at the pastor as he sucked on chicken bones and sopped his fried apples and plopped shad roe cakes into his red cheeks all spiderwebbed with veins. My aunt had to take me into the living room because I fell apart, kicking my legs and trying to pry her hands loose. It was too much to bear in one day. My father came downstairs and sat on the couch beside us. He lifted me from my aunt's arms. "What's the matter?" he asked.

"He . . . (sob) ate . . . (sob) my . . . (sob) roll . . . ," I told him. "The . . . only . . . one . . . I . . . had . . . ."

"We'll get you some more rolls," he said. Well, I knew that would take a while.

My father dug into his pockets and held up a nickel. "This is a brand new coin," he said. "I found it in my change this morning."

I pushed it away. "Can you go and get me a rabbit?" I asked. "You can take that baby back."

My father and my aunt laughed. "No," my father said, "we can't take her back. She belongs to us now and you have to help us take care of her." Tears streamed onto my dress.

"Do you want to see the new baby now?" he asked. As sad as I was, some attention seemed better than none. "But you have to stop crying," he said.

"Okay," I whimpered. He carried me upstairs. My mother was asleep. Her tray of empty dishes was on the dresser. As I looked down into the crib from my father's hip, that baby was asleep, too. I had lost not only my roll of nourishment, but also my role as the baby.

"When she gets bigger, you'll be able to play with her all day long," he said. I hadn't thought of that. This time what he said had a ring of truth to it and soothed me a little. My baby sister did get bigger. Since then, I can't remember a time when I didn't do everything with her or take her everywhere I went. We became best friends. And I did get some more rolls, though, as I predicted, not right away.

My grandmother had begun ailing about the time that my little sister was born, and she died about four years later. Fortunately, my mother had learned to make her mother's rolls, though none of the ingredients were in measured recipe form. It was a sifter full of flour and a pinch of salt from your palm and that sort of thing. My mother still uses my grandmother's sifter and the lard can that she kept her flour in.

Christmastime, my mother sends me rolls. It is March and the remaining ones are still in the freezer. I usually can't bear to throw them out for months.

But I am not sure when I will get any more of my mother's rolls. So I called her to get the recipe: "Sift four and one-half cups of flour (I always use Gold Medal)," my mother said, "with two tablespoons sugar and one teaspoon salt. Scald one and one-half cups milk. That means let it boil up and cut it off. Cut up a quarter stick of margarine or butter and put it in the scalded milk so it will melt. When the milk has cooled, add one beaten egg. But don't let the milk get cold. Now put one and one-half packages of yeast in a bowl or pan and add one-half cup lukewarm water. If the water's too hot, it will kill the yeast and your dough won't rise. Add most of the milk mixture to the yeast mixture and stir it up. I save a little milk back in case I don't need it all. Now put in half the flour and mix it up. Add the other half of flour, a little at a time. Work that up into a soft dough, not sticky. You want it to come off your hands. Then you knead it and knead it. Next, put it in a bowl greased with margarine or butter, and let it rise. This takes about thirty to forty-five minutes. After it has doubled, punch it down and pull off chunks to make them into rolls. I put a dab of softened margarine in the palm of my hand and roll each piece of dough in it. Put the rolls in greased pans. Set them aside to rise again. This takes about twenty to thirty minutes. When they are ready, bake them at 450 degrees until they are light brown. You might only need to set your oven on 400. This recipe makes about three dozen regular dinner rolls," she said.

When I found two and a half hours of uninterrupted time, I made rolls for my family. My son gobbled up three at dinner and got up the next morning and ate one for breakfast.

With that one phone call, and that one afternoon of bread baking, I had moved even farther away from my role as child. I have become the maker of rolls, the comfort giver. The passer of tradition.

ᕦChildren's author Marie Bradby switched from a career as a full-time jour-
nalist to mothering, fiction writing, and freelance writing. She has held staff
reporting positions with the *Providence-Journal* in Rhode Island and, in Kentucky, with the *Lexington Herald-Leader* and the *Courier-Journal*. Bradby was
also a staff writer for *National Geographic Magazine*. Her first book, *More
Than Anything Else*, illustrated by Chris K. Soentpiet, is the winner of the
"1996 IRA Children's Book Award" given by the International Reading Association. It tells the tale of a nine-year-old Booker T. Washington, who, more
than anything else wants to learn to read. This book also has been noted as
an American Library Association Notable Book for Children, *BookLinks* Sa-
lutes a Few Good Books, and the *Chicago Tribune's* Year's Best Books. The PBS
television show, *Storytime*, has produced it as a feature selection.

Leatherbritches

Billy C. Clark

She had been watching the sky for days now looking for a sign. A change in the weather had come. There was a chill in the wind and it carried moisture with it. The sky was as gray as the feathers of a mockingbird. There had been forecasts of cold weather and the possibility of a first snow. But I knew by her searching that she had chosen to follow signs that had been passed down to her by heritage, a heritage that came from her beloved Kentucky hill country. A heritage akin to a birthright.

And then one evening, when the wind had settled as silent as a sunset and flakes of snow fell as soft as bird-down, she said to me:

"I'll put us a mess of Leatherbritches in the kettle to soak tonight.

I'll need a piece of smoked side bacon to season and enough cracklings for cornbread. Soft cracklings, mind you, shed of skin."

To Mom and most of the hill people of the Big Sandy Country, the first mess of Leatherbritches was a yearly ritual that took place with the coming together of two ingredients: The right green bean and the coming of a first snow. Bean-wise, Leatherbritches could only come from a green bean that had strings. Stringless green beans were not considered worth planting in the hill country and were never tolerated. Not then, not now, by true hill country people. Of the string green beans, the mountain white Half Runner has forever been the favorite. The Striped Cornfield Bean and the Old Homestead (Kentucky Wonder) come after. But all three have strings. The latter two are strictly pole beans, with the Half Runner grown either as a bush or pole bean, depending on the preference of the grower. On poles it will grow about half the length of the other two. Thus the name.

In a family of ten, mom and I were the only ones who "took natural to the land." Me, she said, from the time I was hip-carrying size and she could sit me in a furrow for safekeeping while she grubbed out food that we ate in the spring and summer, and put up for the winter by either pickling, drying, or canning.

Our land was plowed each spring by a man by the name of Jess Puckett. He was very old and his back was curved like a hunter's horn. He had a mule that he plowed with named Maud and he brought with him a hillside turning plow that had a spider and coulter on it. He also brought an A-harrow that he had made from wood and railroad spikes and used to level plowed ground. And from an early age I was allowed to ride the harrow since my weight, he said, helped hold it to the ground and I was less work than trying to put a log on it. Plowing or dragging, he never gave the old mule a moment's peace. Cracking a long rawhide whip over her head, he called upon supernatural powers to do her in and cursed her with words that would get you a whipping for even thinking about them. And other words that I was sure would get you a whipping but that I could not find the meaning of anywhere. That is until I was old enough to learn that words like that were also the heritage of hill country people. I mean, whenever you needed a word that you couldn't find to fit the occasion, you just made one yourself. I also learned after I was old enough to work a mule myself that a mule was probably a greater incentive for making new words than anything else in the hill country. But I learned something else about a man and his mule, too. I learned of the special bond that was unbreakable between them. Even between Jess and Maud. For Mom had told me the story of how when the timbers were still big enough up the hollow behind the house to be worth cutting and mule-dragging out, she used to watch Jess stand beside old Maud at the mouth of the hollow with a great log still shackled to her to let her "blow" and cool in the wind that forever came down the hollow. Maud would be frothing at the mouth from the bit and her hide would be lathered with foam-sweat from pulling the log. She stood quivering her hide to shake off the flies that settled on her. Mom had heard him curse her in one breath and then whisper pretty words to her in another while he gave her a handful of soaked corn to eat because she was so old most of her teeth were gone.

Mom laughed. "Ways of menfolk," she said. "Harnesses you to work and figures to wipe it out with a handful of soaked corn."

Mom preferred to raise her Half Runners on short poles. They bore longer and kept their beans off the ground where they were less apt to rot, especially during wet weather. They were also much cleaner. And that was most important when it came to making Leatherbritches since they were never washed before being strung to dry. My job was to get the short poles. And since Mom generally raised a few teepees of Kentucky Wonders for pickling, I needed to get a few long poles, too. Poles usually six or seven feet long from the ground up.

I always got the poles from inside the mouth of the hollow from a sassafras grove that grew on the side of one slope. The tall, slender poles grew like cane, were easy to cut, and would hold well without rotting. Old men claimed that a post-sized sassafras that had been barked would stand seven years as a fence post.

The hollow behind the house was the longest, deepest, and darkest hollow gouged out of the hills at the mouth of the Big Sandy Country. Squeezed by hills on either side, the hollow itself was not much wider than a tramroad. On either side, the slopes were ridged as keen as plow points and looking up appeared high enough to furrow clouds. From these ridges, looking down, the hollow looked no broader than a finger. Scary to look down! But even more scary, I thought, to be standing in the hollow looking up! For the ridges appeared to bend inward threatening to fold over you. And high up old cedars, twisted by winds and whitened by time-death, still clung to cracks in sandstone rocks with gnarled and feeble roots, roots that if whittled on with a pocketknife still held the beautiful red heartwood that Old Timers said would remain for eighty years after the death of the tree. Crows cawed their lonesome songs from ridge to ridge, from cedar to cedar, and turkey buzzards circled above, always searching for something below. And with a boy's imagination, it didn't take much to figure a maybe-what. There were too many scary tales about buzzards to suit me!

Going inside the hollow early of a morning to gather the poles, a fog had generally settled there, and it hung from the limbs of trees like a ghost-wash. As the morning grew old a meager sun came to wring the ghost-wash like the hands of an old woman, and I stopped to listen to it drip, dripping on the underbrush below. Scary and like the tick, ticking of a clock. Moss quilted much of the lowland, and over the mouth of played-out and now-deserted coal belly mines, ice hung like white beards of old men and remained there long after the thaw outside the hollow. What sun there was so early in the spring was as meager as a miner's lamp.

While many of the green beans we raised were eaten fresh, they only served as a prelude to Leatherbritches. Mom's favorite; my favorite! Beans that were used for Leatherbritches were pulled from the vines late in the season when the bean itself inside the shuck was full. Coming just ahead of the first frost, some of the beans had started to dry and had turned a beautiful, almost transparent brownish-yellow. And so the vines held drying beans, green beans, and especially if poled, blooms with a promise they could not keep.

Often Mom and I would pull the vines ahead of frost and doodle them in the yard where we hunkered and stripped the beans from the vines. Pinching off the ends of each bean we pulled the strings "one down the back, one down the belly." I can hear Mom cautioning even today. Mom preferred, generally, to leave the green bean full-length for thread-ing and under no circumstances broken more than once.

I can still see my mother today, her beautiful hair dancing in the wind while she lifted a sewing needle to catch sky-light so she could see to thread the eye with thread she had end-shaped with her teeth and wet with her lips. I can still hear her cautioning me to be sure to sew between beans in the shuck. Once dried, thread through a bean was almost impos-sible to pull out. We sewed the beans into long strings, beading them every few feet with a hot pepper to keep the weevils away. And once threaded, we hung the long strings of beans from the edge of the porch ceiling to dry in the wind and sun. We hung so many that the inside porch was screened off. And you could sit behind the strings on the floor boards of the house and watch as they wind-danced like snakes. The beans would remain on the strings until they had dried to a fraction of their original size. And then they were stripped off the strings and brought inside for winter storage.

To cook, the Leatherbritches were first soaked overnight in a kettle of water, then rinsed and cooked over a low heat the next day until fork-tender. The amount to cook required a cautious and practiced eye. For once touched by water and then heated, Leatherbritches returned to their normal size. And so a mistake here could amount to a boiling over of more beans than pots to hold. The hill country abounded with stories of these mistakes, generally attributed to young brides wanting to please their husbands with their first mess of Leatherbritches fixed away from the watching eyes of their mothers. The mistake made, the best they could hope for was a secret kept. But there were never secrets kept in the hill country, only embellishments added.

Not only was it my job to select enough cracklings for the crackling cornbread, but it was also my job, from an early age, to earn them. For we did not raise hogs. But an old German who lived in the head of the hollow behind the house did; he raised both hogs and hounddogs! Little ones, middle-sized ones, big ones and in-betweens. He was called Old German because it was said that he was as old as the hills and that his nationality was German and you could tell that because he spoke with a German accent although no one I ever knew could tell you what a German accent was supposed to sound like. Truth was, he had a name that you couldn't have pronounced without knowing German, which no one around did, and no one was willing to gamble on a try. Sam Stumbo, who had worked on and off for him more than anyone else, said that the Old German didn't take lightly to having his name mispronounced and that he had creased some poor man's hair some years back with a slug from a hog rifle for doing just that. While some doubted the story, no one cared to find out for sure. I mean, most figured Sam didn't know everything. Asked once where Germany was, he thought a while and said: "Well, it ain't around here."

It was simply reckoned that there was really no need to call him anything anyway. Better to just nod and agree with whatever he said as well as to do whatever he asked, in particular, I figured, if you worked for him on and off, which I did to earn cracklings, smoked slab bacon and the sort, as well as a hounddog pup he held out with a promise, a promise I worried much of the young years of my life about but was afraid to go for a cure and ask.

My job with him amounted to a number of things: feeding hogs as well as helping to raise the feed they ate, making crackling mash to feed his hounds as well as crackling mash to sell to his hunting friends. And when the weather turned cold enough for meat to keep, since the only refrigeration around was ice boxes, my job was to also feed the fires once the hogs were killed so that they could be scalded for scraping. In between feeding the fire, I scraped the hogs with a sharp grubbing hoe alongside three or four men who worked for him and also hunted with him. And while I scraped, I saw each hog drop from the slug of the hog rifle hit between the eyes. I saw the old men drop and wrestle the hog while they slit its throat with a knife they called a pigsticker and catch and drink their fill of the red, hot blood that poured from the slit. Claimed it thickened their own blood to shield against the cold.

After they were scraped and gutted, I cut the fat off them into small chunks and dropped them into a large iron kettle with a fire underneath that I also fed. I stirred the fat to render lard and took payment in cracklings to take home. Cracklings were the residue left from rendering lard and to me the tastiest meat on earth, especially with a little lean meat left on. At best, my take would be cracklings, side bacon that I helped smoke with hickory wood I carried from the slopes, hog heads, pigs' ears, and tails. All of which Mom loved, and except for the smoked side of bacon and cracklings, I tolerated. As a bonus, the Old German allowed me over the winter to sit around the foxfire that I also fed with him and the old men who hunted with him to listen to their hounds and dream of owning my own hound one day, one that would lead the pack.

But many times too tired to join them along the ridge after work, working often from daylight until just this side of dark, I went home by way of crossing the ridge, which saved me more than a mile by not following the hollow out. And most times with my face flushed red by standing over and stirring the hot kettle of cracklings, rendering them for feed and lard, I stopped and looked off down the slope. The embers of the fire seemed no bigger than the glow of a lightning bug. On the ridge the wind was almost unbearable foretelling of a season better to slip away from. Picking my way through briars and brush, along this lonesome ridge the first words of slipping away came: came in the form of a sonnet. The beginning was then, the ending was later. I called it "Creeping from Winter":

Summer is gone and I along this clay
Path pause to watch the hills in winter's mood,

Wind-stripped the naked trees have shook away
My season and now doze in solitude.
Low on the slopes redbud and dogwood bend
From winter's touch, the trailing arbutus
And creeping phlox have sneaked to earthen dens
Leaving their wrinkled trails on frozen crust.
The hills are silent now, and like grey eyes
The mountain rocks are free from summer's green,
Exposed to brightness of a cloudless sky
They blink their freedom from the deep ravine.
I pause to watch, dreaming the while to creep
Away with summer, and from winter sleep.

And from the stirring of a second kettle that held water, cornmeal, and cracklings to make mash for hounds to eat during the winter and on into summer, I gained yet another sonnet that I called "Night of the Singing Hounds":

From high the ridge the hunters stop to play
Cow-horn music to low-singing hounds,
Foxfire ash-covered as the hound of day
Slow-trails the rugged land mouthing no sound.
The song of horn houndtalks an ended night
A ritual song of fox, hound, horn, and men;
Frost-spun the scent of fox is cocoon-tight
To frozen earth that hounds no longer wend.
From high the ridge sore-footed Walkers lag
Their masters down a narrow cow-made trail,
Mute to all boastful talk and hounddog brag
Of bugled voices now on mountain stale.
Night-singing hounds sight-trailing homeward men,
Dreaming of crackling mash and burlap den.

The promise of the Old German for a hounddog pup of my own was never fulfilled. Cracklings for Mom's cornbread were. I am not certain that I would have been willing to have traded the latter for the first. Others raised hounddogs that were just as good hunting-wise as the Old German's. But no one cooked a mess of Leatherbritches and Crackling Cornbread as good eating-wise as Mom.

Leatherbritches

four cups dried shuck beans
enough water to cover beans in kettle
piece of smoked slab bacon
salt (to taste)

Rinse beans in cold water. Cover dried beans with water and soak overnight. Next morning, drain water and rinse beans. Put beans in kettle and cover with water and add a piece of smoked slab bacon. Heat to boiling on high heat and then slow cook until beans are tender. Add salt to taste.

Crackling Cornbread

Preheat oven to 425 degrees. Grease an iron skillet and put it in oven to heat. Sift together:
one cup all-purpose flour
three teaspoons baking powder
one teaspoon salt
pinch of soda
Add:one cup cornmeal (yellow or white) to sifted ingredients
Then add to dry ingredients:
one beaten egg
one and three-fourths cups buttermilk
one cup cracklings

Blend well and pour batter into hot greased iron skillet. Bake twenty to twenty-five minutes at 425 degrees.

∽Billy C. Clark, a native of Catlettsburg, Kentucky, received his B.A. in 1967 from the University of Kentucky. After leaving home to live on his own at age eleven, Clark wrote his autobiography, *Song of the River*, at age fourteen. His thirteen award-winning novels include *Riverboy*, *The Mooneyed Hound*, *The Trail of the Hunter's Horn*, *A Long Row to Hoe*, *Useless Dog*, *Goodbye Kate*, *The Champion of Sourwood Mountain*, and *Sourwood Tales*. In addition to also publishing numerous poems and short stories, Clark served as founding editor of *Kentucky Writing* and *Virginia Writing*. Since 1985 Clark has held the position of writer-in-residence at Longwood College in Farmville, Virginia, where he lives with his wife, Ruth. In 1992 a bridge spanning the Big Sandy River and connecting Kentucky to West Virginia was named the Billy C. Clark Bridge by the state of Kentucky in his honor.

Sweet Potato Balls

MICHAEL DORRIS

My grandmother, Alice Burkhardt, was a woman who guarded her prerogatives. Never wealthy or famous beyond the scope of our family, she nevertheless cloaked herself in an air of dramatic importance: what she said or thought or did, there was no question, mattered, as if each small event was but a metaphor for actions or emotions much larger, more earthshaking than it appeared to the naked eye.

The kitchen was her uncontested domain, and the recipes passed down to her were sacred texts that she never shared even with her own daughters. The role of my mother and aunts was to appreciate her concoctions, to applaud her successes, to marvel at dishes she deigned to produce. Her specialties were few in number but loomed large in legend. Pineapple upside down cake. Chicken fried "just right." A Sunday roast cooked so long and hard that every trace of pink turned gray. Milk gravy.

Nothing, however, competed with the twice-a-year creation (Thanksgiving and Christmas) of a messy-to-make, delicious-to-eat delicacy we knew simply as sweet potato balls. Fat, bright orange, and crusty, with a surprise hidden in their center, these irresistible lumps of high caloric starch punctuated the years as I was growing up.

I'll never forget the Christmas when I came home from college and realized that my grandmother had, as she put it, "slowed down." There was a stiffness to her movements, a hesitancy, that had not been there before. She had suffered from a long bout of flu, my mother explained, but we all knew it was more than that: my grandmother was getting on.

"Let's go out for dinner this year," my aunt suggested with a gaiety she clearly didn't feel. "It's too much work for you, Mama, and I hear the spread at the Holiday Inn is wonderful."

My grandmother seemed for a moment to consider the idea before rejecting it. "You all stay put," she told her two daughters. "Michael will help me cook." Incredulous and curious, I followed her through the swinging door into the holy of holies, and once there she lowered herself onto a chair and began my formal instruction. How to wash, dry, and salt the turkey. How to do the giblets, prepare the celery and sage stuffing, make the cranberry mold, roll the dough for the apple pies. She took me through it all with patience and made me repeat back each step as I was performing it. This was basic training 101, and like all serious traditions, it had to be learned by rote.

Finally we came to the prize, the signature dish, and every time I've made it since, I've heard the directions in her voice, precise and careful, wistful and yet determined. This, and her carved oak bed, was my legacy.

Hours later, when all the dishes were miraculously done at the same time, I carried the steaming plates out to the dining room table and we all took our accustomed places.

"I can't believe my eyes," my aunt said. "Even the sweet potato balls."

"They came out good this year," my grandmother commented—though usually she said just the opposite in order to be strenuously contradicted. "Michael is a quick study."

My mother and aunt looked at me, and I at them. We all knew that the torch had been passed, that from now on Thanksgiving and Christmas dinner would be mine to make.

Sweet Potato Balls

Boil (until breakable with a fork) in lightly salted water six large sweet potatoes, peeled and sliced into one-inch rounds. Drain. With a potato masher
(or a strong electric mixer) whip the softened potatoes together with about a
half-cup of heavy cream, a quarter-cup of brown sugar, a good splash of maple
syrup, a half-cup of chopped walnuts, a dash of vanilla, a splash of bourbon
or cognac, salt and pepper to taste. Using an ice-cream scoop (or your hand),
gather a clump of the mixture and form it around a large marshmallow, then
roll the ball in crushed cornflakes or cornflake crumbs; continue until all
potatoes are used up. Set balls several inches apart on slightly oiled aluminum foil spread on cookie sheet. Bake at 350 degrees for approximately twenty
minutes, then top each ball with a second marshmallow and put under broiler
until it's slightly browned and melting.

My grandmother was an instinctive cook and rarely measured her ingredients precisely. Everything should be considered approximations, altered
according to taste and mood.

~Michael Dorris (1945-1997) was born in Louisville, Kentucky, and spent
much of his childhood in the Crescent Hill section of the city, attending Holy
Spirit grade school and St. Xavier High School. He was a graduate of
Georgetown and Yale Universities; held Danforth, Woodrow Wilson, and
Guggenheim fellowships; and founded the Native American Studies Depart-
ment at Dartmouth College (where he taught for fourteen years). He authored
thirteen books, both fiction and nonfiction, including three novels for young
adults. Among his best known works are *A Yellow Raft in Blue Water* (1987),
The Broken Cord (1989), *Morning Girl* (1992), *Sees Behind Trees* (1996) and
Cloud Chamber (1997).

A Child's Garden of Memories

JOHN EGERTON

Some things are easier to remember than others. I may have a hard time thinking of the name of a song—but play me a couple of bars, and suddenly I'll recall the tune and most of the lyrics. You may be good at names, while I never forget a face. Shapes may activate my recall button, while yours works best on colors.

And then there is food, the most evocative element of all. The reason is obvious: It can be called to mind through all five of the senses. Your nose will draw you irresistibly to a simmering pot of beans; you can hear the sizzle of bacon in a skillet, feel the fuzz on a tree-ripened peach, see the beauty of a Thanksgiving table—and of course you can savor the unforgettable taste of everything from a bowl of chicken soup to a slice of chocolate meringue pie.

To illustrate my point, let me tell you a tale about a summer supper—a true story that recaptures an afternoon and evening of outdoor dining some fifty years ago, when I was a boy of about ten. The scene is still quite vivid in my mind. To the backyard of our home in a rural Kentucky town, my mother had invited a small multitude of relatives and friends for an informal dinner. In truth, it was a banquet. This is how I remember it:

I'm guessing that it was late August in the summer of 1945 or '46, shortly after the war ended. The opening of school, a perennial day of dread for footloose kids like me, was a brooding shadow hovering at the edge of my consciousness. Recalling that season now, I can hear Benny Goodman's sweet clarinet playing "September Song," plaintive and wistful—a lament for the days that do indeed grow short, and always too soon. Time for just one more summer fling, one more harvest feast.

The food we grew and prepared and ate in those days—our daily bread, our jug of tea, our meat and greens, our sweet everythings—was far more than just sustenance; it had social as well as nutritional value. Food was in the forefront of our daily routines. It was in large measure our work and our play; no wonder it's a primary source of memories.

Out in the backyard, under a maple tree near one corner of the garden, our resourceful and trowel-handy mother had built an outdoor grill of stone and mortar—the first I had ever seen, and a forerunner of the portable patio models to come. In celebration of its completion and of the garden's rich but dwindling bounty, she announced a Saturday afternoon feast, and to that end we all directed our thoughts and energies—parents and siblings, elders and youngsters, aunts and uncles and cousins, probably twenty of us altogether.

We had a long-established family practice of raising chickens for both the eggs and the meat—baked hen as the mainstay for Sunday dinner, and tender young pullets fried in hot lard at least once or twice a week. On this occasion there would be something new for us: marinated chicken halves cooked over hardwood coals on the new grill.

Becka (the name our other relatives commonly called Mother) started on Friday by coaxing a dozen of the feathered fleet to her chopping block, one by one, and dispatching them quickly with swift swings of her razor-sharp hatchet. We then plucked the feathers and watched her as she cut the birds into symmetrical halves and refrigerated them in salted ice water.

The next day, while the bed of coals was being readied, Becka prepared a spicy marinade and basting sauce and put the chicken halves in it to soak up flavor. Later, when they went onto the grill, the novelty of this process made us acutely attentive. It was right here that all your senses kicked in: the pungent, mingled aromas of the sauce, the woodsmoke, and the cooking meat; the tantalizing sight and sound as it slowly turned golden-brown and crispy before your very eyes; the too-hot-to-handle lure of it on the platter; and finally, the incredibly fresh and tangy flavor of it once you took that first bite.

But I'm getting ahead of the story. The garden was my bittersweet field of daydreams, at once an infernal purgatory of endless rows to be hoed and an Eden of unforbidden deliciousness. Out of it came all the raw ingredients from which Becka and her helpers would create our selection of side dishes.

The cold ones first: crunch-crisp cucumbers and onions in salted vinegar-water; sliced beefsteak tomatoes, their vine-ripened acidity perfectly complemented by homemade mayonnaise and cottage cheese; new potatoes and bell peppers and green onions for the potato salad.

And then the hot ones: yellow crookneck squash baked in a bubbly casserole with onions, garlic, milk, cheese, eggs, and bread crumbs; shelled butterbeans (or was it field peas?) simmered to tender perfection in a little water, with a chunk of side meat tossed in for added flavor. And two more, the alpha and omega of southern vegetables, the ying and yang of garden mysticism: Silver Queen, a divine variety of white-kernel sweet corn (roasting ears, in the vernacular), and Kentucky Wonder pole beans, the highest order of green vegetables in the culinary orbit. (It may be that these are newer varieties that weren't available then—memory does play tricks on you sometimes—but they seem ageless and immortal to me now.)

Preparation of the roasting ears was the soul of simplicity, and for that reason they came last to the groaning board. When the guests were gathered at our makeshift banquet tables on the lawn and the blessing had been said, Becka brought her huge kettle of water to a rolling boil on the stove. She then signaled for my brother and me to go for the corn.

We rushed down the rows, ripping off ears with both hands; others pitched in to peel off the shucks and silks, and as soon as the ears were ready, we dropped them into the boiling cauldron for no more than ten minutes, and then put one on each plate. Talk about fresh, and sweet!

The pole beans got an earlier start, of course. We picked a huge mess of them (a mess being an imprecise unit of measure equal to enough). They had to be stringed, snapped, washed, and cooked for a couple of hours or more in a big black kettle, moistened with a small amount of water and seasoned with salt and a piece of side meat (by whatever name, simply pork). The beans came out blue-green, limp, luminous with the essence of porcine flavoring—and indescribably delicious.

Cornbread muffins were in unlimited supply for the hand opposite your fork. They were baked by the dozen in fluted irons and kept warm in the oven. The obligatory drink was iced tea, freshly brewed and poured up into gallon jugs, then passed around and augmented with individual measures of sugar, lemon, and mint.

The final glories of Becka's feast were piping-hot cobblers in three varieties: blackberry, peach, and cherry. The fruits had come from country briar thickets and orchards earlier in the summer and been "put up" (canned or dried) for just such occasions as this. The cobblers emerged from the oven delicately encased in a latticework of crust, and they soon disappeared without a trace.

The six major food groups in southern cooking back then were sugar, cream, butter, eggs, salt, and pork fat. There wasn't much knowledge or consciousness of cancer, heart attacks, and strokes, and the word "cholesterol" was utterly unknown to us—if, indeed, it had ever been coined. Life expectancy was much shorter than it is today, but the reasons aren't entirely clear; while some people died much too young, others lived for a century in robust good health, and more often than not they did so on diets heavy with the Big Six.

What may have saved those lucky ones, besides a favorable genetic heritage and a more active and vigorous lifestyle, was the absence of synthetically produced, chemically treated, multi-processed, microwave-zapped, artificial, unattractive, tasteless food in their daily diet. We have not yet unraveled the mysteries of what we eat and what it does for us and to us, but I can tell you from empirical knowledge that traditional southern cooking had many virtues, not least among them being the profound sense of mental and physical well-being it so often gave to those who partook.

I'm not sure what summer suppers like the feast I've described did to us healthwise, but I do know what they did for us. A meal like this was a social act, a communion with nature and with kinfolk, an expression of love and generosity. We drew much more than physical nourishment from it; this was food for the soul and the spirit as well. It touched every facet of my senses, and touches them still. In the waning days of every summer, the "September Song" days, I bring those treasures of yesterday's cookery to mind—and even, once in a while, to the stove and the table.

Barbecue Sauce

The marinade and basting sauce recipe came from the University of Kentucky Poultry Department. One of its many virtues was that it gave meat (not just chicken but pork too) a golden finish, crisp and crusty on the outside but never burned. Tomato is the barbecue sauce ingredient that causes meat to burn, and this mixture contained no tomato products. It was—and is—a superlative sauce. This is the formula:

In a large saucepan, combine the following: Two and one-half cups water, one tablespoon sugar, two and one-half teaspoons black pepper, two tablespoons vegetable oil, one-fourth cup cider vinegar, two and one-half teaspoons salt, two tablespoons Worcestershire sauce, one small onion minced fine, one teaspoon powdered mustard, one-half teaspoon hot pepper sauce, one clove garlic minced fine, one-half teaspoon red pepper, and two teaspoons chili powder. Stir and simmer for a few minutes over low heat, letting the diversity of flavors blend into a medley of spicy hotness.

And that's it. This amount—about three cups—is enough to marinate and baste four to six small birds, halved. Pour the cooled mixture over the meat a couple of hours before cooking, and then baste generously during the grilling process.

Cornbread Muffins

The recipe was a nineteenth-century heirloom from Tennessee. For each dozen, this was the method:

Mix together one cup plain white cornmeal, three tablespoons all-purpose flour, one teaspoon baking powder, one-fourth teaspoon salt, and one-fourth teaspoon baking soda. In a separate bowl, combine one whole egg and one cup buttermilk, and stir this liquid into the dry mixture. Then add two tablespoons melted bacon grease (or other shortening). Grease the irons, get them smoking hot in a 475-degree oven, and quickly fill them with the batter. Rush to the oven for about twelve minutes, or until golden brown and crusty on top.

Blackberry Cobbler

The beginning of the confection was a pastry for a big six-by-twelve-inch baking dish (it took two of these for our crowd). To two cups all-purpose flour were added one teaspoon salt, one-third pound (that's one and one-third sticks) of unsalted butter (no substitutes), and some ice water (six or seven tablespoons, added a little at a time). The flour and salt were sifted together, and the butter was cut into it with a pastry blender; then the water was added until the dough was well moistened and could be gathered into a ball. This was chilled, and then a little more than half of it was rolled out on a floured surface like pie pastry and the well-greased baking dish was lined with it, taking care to cover the sides and corners.

Next, at least six full cups of blackberries were well mixed with one and one-fourth cups sugar and two tablespoons cornstarch. This mixture was poured into the pastry dish, and the remaining pastry was rolled out, cut into strips, and criss-crossed over the top. Finally, another five or six tablespoons of butter cut into thin patties were dotted all over the top. The dish went into a 425-degree oven for fifteen minutes, after which the temperature was reduced to 375 degrees and the baking continued for about forty-five more minutes. The cobbler came out beautifully encased in a latticework of crust, with the berries a cauldron of sweet juiciness.

～Trigg County, Kentucky, native John Egerton, who currently lives in Nashville, Tennessee, holds two degrees from the University of Kentucky and an honorary doctorate from Berea College. His books include *Generations*, *Speak Now Against the Day*, *Southern Food*, and *Side Orders*. A version of this essay first appeared in the July-August, 1996, issue of *Modern Maturity*.

Sunday Cooking

Jane Gentry

My grandfather was a hellfire and damnation preacher. I'm as puzzled now, fifty years later, as I was as a child by how he could be so frightening and, at the same time, such a figure of fun, his blue eyes shining as he teasingly accused me, a good girl, of throwing rocks at the school bus. He was the pattern of contradiction, preaching righteousness and playing the devil with his grandchildren. Every Sunday at eleven a.m. church, he took a vivid text. One of his favorites he called "The Valley of the Dead, Dry Bones," and he concluded that recitation (The Book of Ezekiel, 37) with reference to passages in "The Book of Isaiah," the fieriest and therefore his favorite prophet, as in chapter 47, verse 14: "Behold, they shall be as stubble; the fire shall burn them; they shall not deliver themselves from the power of the flame: there shall not be coal to warm at, nor fire to sit before it." I never got my mind around the logic of the last bit, but I clearly understood that it meant more flame to eat me alive.

After the reading of the text and the telling of an illustrative anecdote, often drawn from one of his visits to the deathbed of an alcoholic or a prostitute, or to the wake of an unrepentant sinner, in mounting crescendos of metaphor and (I hope) hyperbole, he would paint a picture of the future of those of us there present who were not saved. Since I had not put off the "Old Man," shed the "Old Adam" like a snake bursts out of its skin, and had not put on the "New Man," the shining garments of Jesus Christ, and thus had not entered the Sonhood of God, then I would burn for ten thousand thousand years (and then start over again) in the great lake of Hellfire.

Now as a girl-child, five to seven years old, I knew I had never been changed into the "New Man," nor had I any inkling how I could be the "Old Adam," who went naked except for leaves and did as instructed by Eve, who got her wisdom from a walking snake. I felt no kinship with this person, and so I knew I had not accepted Jesus as my personal savior, the lord of my life. As hard as I tried to feel it (but Grandaddy said over and over that it could not be willed), I could not: that great second birth which would conduct me out of my damned body, and deposit me, gloriously regenerated, at the foot of God's throne, high on a bank of billowing backlit clouds, with a golden river flowing in front of it.

All I could be sure of was that I was not saved, but that I had reached the dread "Age of Accountability," which Grandaddy reckoned at around age seven. I knew I had reached it because I was under conviction of my sins, and was therefore eligible for the Lake of Fire in which Satan himself paced unscathed, wielding a pitchfork, just like the one my father pitched hay to his cattle with, to prod back into the red flames any sinner who tried to escape.

I knew I had reached this doomed age because I was ashamed, just as, so Grandaddy said, Adam and Eve were upon being discovered naked in the Garden. My cheeks had burned when my most morally certain aunt had called me down at my cousin's birthday party for saying, when she asked me if I wanted chocolate, strawberry, or vanilla ice cream with my cake, "It doesn't matter to me. Whichever you have most of." My failure to know and state my preference was not a Christian transgression, because, after all, what I said was "unselfish," but nevertheless my sense was acute that I had fallen short of the glory in some important way. Shame was an equal opportunity emotion. And I knew it was a sin that ever since the birth of my little brother I had dreams that I liked about pushing fat baby boys out of second-story windows, and about pinching their pink flesh.

So I knew I was going to Hell, guilty as a harlot or a moneychanger, unredeemed. I had been sure I would be saved by the time I started school. When the magical transformation still didn't take place, when I was six, I hit on the strategem of keeping down my fear by rubbing my hands over my ears during the climactic passages of Grandaddy's sermons. Sometimes, when I could see that his mouth had stopped, that he was no longer pounding the cushioned top of the lectern, that he was no longer baring his teeth in fierce articulation, I would still my palms for a moment, only to be pierced by the invitation hymn: "Just as I am, without one plea, except that Jesus died for me; O Lamb of God, I come, I come." Only I didn't. My six-months-older, spiritually advanced second cousin had been converted when she was only five and one-half. So I knew I was lost forever, that I had somehow committed the mysterious "Unpardonable Sin." But sometimes the song was my favorite, the less frightening: "Shall we gather at the river, the beautiful, the beautiful river, gather with the saints at the river, that flows past the throne of God." My Mother would be there, my beloved Maugie would be there, all my aunts would be there, my second cousin would be there, and Grandaddy, of course, would be there at God's own right hand. Only I, I felt in those moments, of all the people whose shoes stood on the brown linoleum of the auditorium, would not be there. I would be burning, screaming in Hell.

After church we would all go to Maugie and Grandaddy's house just two blocks away, on Aurora Avenue, for Sunday dinner. Grandaddy was exhausted from herding all us sinners into the strait gate that led away from that burning place. He got home later than the rest of us, delivered by a faithful deacon to the back door. He went immediately to his daybed and fell, without saying a word, into a deep sleep.

The beef roast had been cooking in the Dutch oven for at least two hours by now and filled the house with delicious, fatty smells. About ten minutes before the meat was to be drawn from the oven, falling apart in its steamy tenderness, Maugie shook him gently, "Daddy, daddy, time to eat."

Up from his bed he arose, went straight to the kitchen and opened a small can of sauerkraut, which he took for his digestion. He ate all the wormy contents and then drank off the odorous juice. He came to the dining room table, where at least four of his seven grandchildren and two of his three daughters, already seated, starving after the rigors of sitting through his sermon, waited for him to say grace:

"Bless this food to the nourishment of our bodies and us to thy holy service. Forgive us our sins and lead us into the paths of righteousness. All this we ask in Jesus's name and for his sake. Amen."

My place was on the side of the table facing the buffet that now sits in my dining room. Over it hung, in birth order, with me at the beginning, baby portraits of all seven of his grandchildren. We looked at our pictures there and knew that we belonged, in our relations each to the other, when we could only see over the edge of the buffet on tiptoes. In 1969 when his daughters had to take them down, after he died, my heart protested that the pictures couldn't be separated, that they at least had to stay together, and hang on another wall, in their hierarchy that gave us each a place in the house of our grandfather, who was the harbinger of our damnation and our salvation.

Nobody needed or relished more than he, ascetic though his theology was, the comfort of the succulent roast beef, with the dark rich gravy poured over the potatoes already saturated in the broth. He appreciated, too, and always complimented Maugie on, the zest of the slaw, or the sweet cloudiness of the angel food cake with its white sugar icing, or the amber-beaded butterscotch meringue pie.

For a man who abhorred the appetites of the flesh, he, along with the rest of the variously unaccountable and unsaved, enjoyed it all. He ate his food, in its own way as saving, as refreshing as the Lord's Supper itself, gratefully, ritualistically, and fairly neatly, but always with a dish towel tied under his chin, complimenting Maugie as he went, and cleaning the plates of any children who left scraps.

Even his fixing me with his water-blue eyes during the meal and asking me why I had thrown rocks at the school bus during the week did not upset my comfort at this feast of safety and pleasure, so far did I feel from the hard benches of the church and fiery figures of his sermon.

When the last child had been granted permission to push back from the table and return to play in the sandbox or in the jungle of the neighbor's cutting, ornamental grasses, Grandaddy took up his place at the kitchen sink, with Maugie's apron tied over the mound of his satisfied belly, and shooing his wife and daughters from the room, he would slowly re-order the kitchen, talking to himself in the mirror over the sink, as if his image there were a real and critical presence. I often heard him laugh with himself; sometimes he seemed despairing. Always he seemed to me to be talking about the souls he tried to save, the ones, like me, he failed to save, but would never, ever give up on.

Sunday Roast Beef

three-to-four pound chuck roast
eight medium-size potatoes
four carrots
two stalks of celery
two medium-size onions
two beef bouillon cubes
Worcestershire sauce
tomato ketchup

Dissolve two bouillon cubes in two cups water. Lightly salt and thoroughly pepper the roast, top and bottom. Brown it on both sides in a skillet over medium heat. Place it in a large Dutch oven (roasting pan) and add bouillon mix. Add hot water until it comes three-quarters up the roast.

Put one tablespoon Worcestershire sauce on top of roast. Put one tablespoon tomato ketchup on top of roast.

Place quartered onions on top of roast. Place, covered, in oven at 300 degrees for two and one-half hours, or (for increased tenderness) at 275 degrees for three to four hours. After the roast has cooked for one hour, place potatoes, carrots, and celery in liquid around it. Re-cover tightly.

Gravy

Place the Dutch oven on a stove burner. Remove vegetables and meat and arrange on a platter. Dip half a cup of broth from the Dutch oven into a cup. Sprinkle cornstarch into this bit of broth and mix in well. Add this mixture gradually to the broth left in the Dutch oven. Stir vigorously from the bottom of the pan, until the gravy reaches the desired consistency. Add a little water if you need to stretch the gravy, and add more cornstarch for greater thickness. Sinners and Saved alike will delight in this flesh thoroughly roasted in its own juice!

∾Jane Gentry, a Lexington, Kentucky native, now lives in Versailles, Kentucky. She holds a B.A. from Hollins College, an M.A. from Brandeis University where she was a Woodrow Wilson Fellow, and a Ph.D. in English and American literature from the University of North Carolina at Chapel Hill. A professor in the English Department and Honors Program at the University of Kentucky, Gentry is also a founding coordinator of the University of Kentucky Women Writers Conference. Her poems and critical essays have appeared in *Harvard Magazine, The American Voice, New Virginia Review, Hollins Critic, Sewanee Review, Southern Poetry Review, Humanities in the South, America, Journal of Kentucky Studies, Southern Literary Journal,* and numerous other journals and anthologies. Gentry's collection of poetry, *A Garden in Kentucky,* was published by Louisiana State University Press in 1995.

A Fig-Flavored Visit
with Eudora Welty

WADE HALL

One of the most anticipated pleasures of my boyhood in South Alabama was the late-summer ripening of the figs on the trees in our backyard. We called them trees because they were taller than me or any of my four younger brothers. Indeed, we frequently had to climb them to pick off the most succulent ones from the top branches. Occasionally, we would slip and skin our arms and legs, but the risk was worth the reward.

And what a reward it was! Light-brown, almost purple, fruit that tasted like it was straight from the orchards of Paradise. We were tempted to eat them straight off the tree—and, in fact, we did. We'd brush the gnats, ants, flies, and birds away from the fruit and plop them ravenously into our mouths.

How can I describe that exquisite taste? Imagine the creamiest ice cream, the velvetiest cake, the most sumptuous pie you've ever eaten—all blended by angelic chefs—and you'll have some notion of what my mother's five little boys were tasting up in those delectable trees.

But fresh figs do not last all year long. Within a few weeks the limbs of the fig trees would be plucked of all their fruit—by nature, by lucky birds, and by the eager hands of family and friends. Some of the fruit was harvested to be cooked into preserves in my grandmother's giant kettles. It was a table delight almost matching the fresh fruit. Well do I remember the buckets of figs that, first my grandmother, then my mother—with insistent aid from little hands—would rinse in well water, peel partially, and place, covered with sugar, in the large cooking pots. Usually, the figs would be stripped of their stems before adding the sugar and placing them on the wood-burning stove. Sometimes, however, the stems and skins would be left intact, thus providing a handy holder for eating the preserved fig.

Short lengths of hickory or pine wood—stovewood, we called it—were added to the firebox on the stove's left side, and soon the kitchen and indeed the entire house were suffused with fig-flavored aroma. At just the right moment, after about forty or fifty minutes, the cooked figs were removed and ladled into the already sterilized jars waiting in a pan of boiling water. After the lids and rings were placed on the jars—so many pints and so many quarts—and tightened, they were placed on the canned-goods table in the southwest corner of the dining room, where they joined dozens of jars of tomatoes, beans, field peas, corn, beets, peaches, and other fruits and vegetables that would feed our eager appetites through the lean, cold months.

The jars of fig preserves were considered special treats and were not for everyday consumption. A fresh jar was opened on certain occasions—like when company or the preacher came, or at Thanksgiving and Christmas. We boys liked to eat them like candy straight from the jar, but more often they were placed inside fresh buttered biscuits as a breakfast or supper treat. With care and rationing, the canned preserves could stretch from one harvest to the next.

Living in Kentucky, a bit north of the fig culture, for more than thirty years, I have missed the annual harvest, though I have occasionally been fortunate enough to visit my family in Alabama at the opportune time and participate in the fig gathering and preserving ritual.

Several years ago, a few months after my mother's death in April of 1990, I drove to Alabama with friends in early July during the peak of the fig season. Enlisting their aid, I gathered enough figs from my late mother's two fig trees to provide several rounds of fresh desserts as well as six quarts of preserves. Now we get to the Eudora Welty Connection. One of those jars was soon destined to claim a space in Miss Welty's pantry some two hundred miles due west in Jackson, Mississippi.

We had planned to drive back to Kentucky by way of Mississippi, a detour of perhaps 350 miles that would lead us through Montgomery, Selma, and Demopolis, Alabama, and across the state line into Meridian, through Jackson, and over to Vicksburg, thence up through the Mississippi Delta to Memphis, Tennessee, and finally into Western Kentucky. Jackson is, of course, the Mississippi state capital and, more importantly, the home of one of America's best living writers, Eudora Welty, with whom I've been carrying on an occasional correspondence since 1970, when *Losing Battles*, her masterpiece of fiction, was published. At that time I was serving as a kind of unofficial southern reviewer-in-residence for The *Courier-Journal*, and my review of her novel appeared in the May 10, 1970, issue. The following week I received a letter from Miss Welty, dated May 18, which read:

Dear Dr. Hall,

I'd like you to know how much I value your review of my new book in The *Courier-Journal & Times*, and how grateful I am for your perceptions and the generosity of your remarks. I felt that you had such clear sight of what I was aiming for, and of how I was trying to get there, as near as I could. Thank you for what you wrote.

I owe Mr. Jesse Stuart for kindly mailing me the clipping from the paper. He'd scribbled across the top "Excellent review" and I agree with that.

Sincerely,
Eudora Welty

Needless to say, I was ecstatic over her unsolicited endorsement of my critical acumen! She was already very high on my hit parade of "Best Living American Authors," and after her letter she quickly rose to the Number One spot. Following her first letter to me, I tried periodically to lure her to Bellarmine College, where I was teaching, to do a reading. Each time she politely declined. In a letter dated March 18, 1974, she explained that she had stopped visiting schools to lecture and read because such work "keeps me from doing my real work of writing."

Although I have been a fan of Miss Welty's writing since high school and college, I had never met her or seen her in person. When it was obvious that our trip back to Kentucky would lead through Jackson and within a mile or so of her home on Pinehurst Street, I decided to strike boldly—without sounding too forward—and ask if we might stop by for a brief visit. Accordingly, I wrote her shortly before we left Louisville and gave her my Alabama address. The day before we were to leave Halls Cross Road on our circuitous return trip to Kentucky through Mississippi, I received this letter from her:

> Dear Mr. Hall,
> If was nice to hear from you. If you will take me as you find me, in a torn-up house and in all this heat, then do come by. Could you call before you come, and I'll tell you how to get here . . .
>
> > Yours sincerely,
> > Eudora Welty
>
> Thanks for the offer of lunch but I am in the middle of working & would enjoy just seeing you here in the early afternoon as you mentioned.
>
> > E.

The next day we left my family home so early we arrived in Jackson well before noon. After driving around sightseeing for an hour and more, we stopped at a public phone and I called Miss Welty's number. She gave me directions and we easily made our way to Pinehurst Street near downtown. Soon I stopped at her 1920s Gothic Revival home at 1119 Pinehurst and spotted her 1972 Dodge sitting in the driveway with its '88 Dukakis bumper sticker still proudly displayed.

Miss Welty was waiting for us at the door in a multi-hued blue and pink "company" dress and ushered us into her living room to the left of the hall. Fortunately, the extreme heat had been broken by summer rains, and through the open windows a light breeze stirred. She showed us to seats around the room, and she settled herself in a large blue overstuffed chair that appeared to be the vintage of the house. The room and fireplace were framed in dark mahogany woodwork, and French doors opened into the dining room. Despite several unopened boxes in one corner— brought, she said, from an upstairs room—the room seemed uncluttered, even sparsely furnished. She explained that her "torn-up house" was the result of her doctor's orders to move her bedroom/study downstairs because of her worsening arthritis. "I have great difficulty," she said, "going up and down the steps."

For some two hours we talked about her work and we told her of our favorite stories "Why I Live at the P.O.," "Petrified Man," "A Still Moment," "A Worn Path," "The Wide Net." I had recently seen the television version of "The Wide Net" and told her how well I thought the story was adapted. She disagreed. "The outdoor scenes," she said, "were filmed near the coast and not on their actual locale on the Pearl River near Jackson. Furthermore, the producers used my name in raising funds for the project. I disliked that very much." Steering the conversation away to a more pleasant subject, I mentioned our mutual fondness for North Carolina writer Reynolds Price. "Yes," she said, "I like Reynolds and his work very much." Despite her debility, she said she planned to attend an upcoming dinner and awards ceremony in his honor.

In typical southern fashion, we chatted on for much longer than I had intended. I apologized for intruding on her for so long, but she said she was used to it. She told us about the many books she received each week from readers wanting autographs. "Then," she said in a mildly complaining voice, "I have to box them up again and take them down to the post office." She added, "There are also the frequent strangers who appear unannounced at my doorstep. I try to be polite to them, but I must have time for my work." At least, I thought, we asked if we could come and she said yes.

Finally, I said, "Miss Welty, we must not take up any more of your time. But it's getting late and we'd be delighted to take you out for dinner." She declined because of a prior commitment to friends. Then, as we stood up to go, I said, "Miss Welty, how would you like a jar of fig preserves? I've just made some off my mother's trees in Alabama." She said, "Oh, that would be lovely, but can you spare a whole jar?" I said, "Why, there's one with your name on it in the back seat of my car." As she and my two friends were saying goodbye, I rushed out to get a jar of fig preserves and a camera. She agreed to sign a couple of books before we left and allowed me to take several pictures of her in her chair and in her doorway as we were leaving. In a couple of the photographs she is holding my "lovely" gift. As we turned off Pinehurst Street, we were lighter by one jar of fig preserves but bubbling happily over our extraordinary visit to one of the grand literary icons of our time.

I later worried that with her arthritic hands she might have trouble opening the tightly sealed jar of preserves. But I remembered that she had told us she had someone who came in to cook and do her housework. Presumably, her hands were strong enough to open up the jar of fig preserves. At least, I could imagine Miss Eudora Welty sitting at her dining room table on a cold winter morning and enjoying my homemade fig preserves in a hot, buttered biscuit.

My mother and grandmother, who over their lifetimes canned thousands of jars of fruits and vegetables and berries, never cooked or canned from written recipes. They learned to make up biscuits by watching and imitating their elders until the process became second nature to them. That's the way they learned to prepare all the other tasty country foods of my boyhood, from chicken dressing and country ham to pecan cakes and dried-peach tarts. I don't ever remember seeing a recipe book in my boyhood home. But I am a child of another generation, and I learned to cook from books. The following fig recipes, therefore, are gleaned and adapted from the several dozen cookbooks that are as essential to my kitchen as the refrigerator and the range. Whatever extra touches these recipes have, however, come from my memories of two country women who spent much of their lives cooking for husbands and children who realized too late how fortunate they were.

Figs and Cream

Let's begin with a simple one, "Figs and Cream," a dish that no one had to teach me. Instinctively, I knew that plump ripe figs picked fresh from the tree would be enhanced by taking them inside to chill, then sprinkling sugar and pouring rich cream over them. The only problem with this dessert is that you can never make enough.

Almond-Stuffed Figs

A rather elegant way to prepare figs is "Almond-Stuffed Figs" or "Bon-bons de Figos," an after-dinner treat usually served with a glass of port. One advantage to this recipe is that you don't have to have a fig tree outside your back door. Most large food stores stock the dried figs you will need:

one-half cup whole blanched almonds
one pound dried figs

Preheat the oven to 350 degrees. Spread the almonds evenly in a baking dish and toast them in the oven until lightly browned, about ten minutes, turning them occasionally. Remove from oven and chop half the almonds coarsely. Set all almonds aside to cool.

Cut off stems from figs. Chop the figs coarsely, then puree them through a food mill. To make each bonbon, butter the palms of your hands and roll about one teaspoon of the pureed figs into a ball. Insert a whole almond into the ball and shape it until the nut is completely enclosed. Then roll the bon-bon in the chopped almonds to coat thoroughly and set aside on wax paper. Follow this procedure for the remaining figs and almonds to make about thirty. Preserved figs don't have to be eaten in hot, buttered biscuits. Here's another way to use your canned treat as an hors d'oeuvre.

Bishop's Hat Fig Surprise

one pound dried figs
two cups of flour
two teaspoons of red pepper
one cup of grated sharp cheddar cheese
one stick of butter or margarine

Blend the cheese and butter until it's orange and not lumpy. Add two tea-spoons of red pepper and three tablespoons of cold water and mix thoroughly. Roll out like a pie crust on a floured board and cut into three-inch triangles or squares. Place a fig preserve in the middle of each piece. Then fold points to the center over the fig. Dampen the edges with milk and pinch together like a bishop's hat. Bake on an ungreased sheet in a 350-degree oven for about twenty minutes or until golden brown. Serve hot with cocktails. You can do just about anything with figs that you can do with other fruits, includ-ing pickling them. This recipe is sometimes called "Louisiana Pickled Figs," but in this recipe we'll name them after Kentucky.

Kentucky Pickled Figs

one and one-half quarts of ripe figs
three cups of sugar
one-half cup of vinegar
one tablespoon broken cinnamon sticks
one tablespoon whole cloves

Cover figs in one quart of boiling water. Let stand for five minutes and drain. Mix one-half cup of water with vinegar and sugar in a large saucepan. Add spices in a bag. Bring to boil and add figs. Boil for ten minutes. Let stand until the next day; then boil again for ten minutes. Let stand another day; then boil again for ten minutes. Remove spice bag and pack in sterile jars. Yield: Two pints. Next is a modified fruitcake recipe which is popular around Thanksgiving and Christmas.

Fig Preserve Cake

one and one-half cups of sugar
two cups of all-purpose flour
one teaspoon of baking soda
one teaspoon of salt
one teaspoon of ground nutmeg
one teaspoon of ground cinnamon
one-half teaspoon of ground allspice
one-half teaspoon of ground cloves
one cup of vegetable oil
three eggs
one cup of buttermilk
one tablespoon of vanilla extract
one cup of chopped fig preserves
one-half cup of chopped pecans

Combine all dry ingredients in a large bowl. Add oil. Beat well. Add eggs and beat well. Add buttermilk and vanilla and mix thoroughly. Stir in the preserves and pecans. Pour batter into greased and floured ten-inch tube pan. Bake at 350 degrees for one hour and fifteen minutes. Let cool for ten minutes and remove from pan. Pour the following glaze over the warm cake.

Buttermilk glaze

Mix one-fourth cup of buttermilk, one-half cup of sugar, one and one-half teaspoons of cornstarch, and one-fourth cup of margarine and bring to a boil. Remove from heat. Cool slightly and stir in vanilla. Pour glaze on warm cake. Yum! Yum!

By adding figs to orange marmalade, you can make a condiment fit for the gods.

Fig Marmalade

two lemons, thinly sliced
two pounds of fresh figs
two oranges, grated rind and juice
two pounds of sugar

Simmer lemon slices in water in a small saucepan until tender. Drain. Chop figs and combine with grated rind, juice of two oranges, and sugar in a large pot. Bring to a boil and cook over a low heat for fifteen minutes, stirring occasionally. Add drained lemons and continue to cook slowly until thick. Seal in hot sterile jars.

I don't think Baskin-Robbins has discovered fig ice cream yet, but when they do, watch out vanilla, chocolate, and rocky road! Here's a simple way to make a different kind of ice cream, which we will name after my native state.

Alabama Fig Ice Cream

one cup of sugar
two cups of finely chopped fresh figs
two teaspoons of lemon juice
two cups of light cream

Pour the sugar over the fresh figs and let stand one-half hour. Then run through a colander and add the lemon juice to bring out the flavor. Add two cups of light cream. Freeze in a crank freezer. Yield: Six servings.

Finally, here is the granddaddy of all fig recipes.

Fig Preserves

six cups of stemmed and chopped figs
one thinly sliced lemon
three cups of sugar

Combine the figs, lemon, and sugar in a heavy stainless-steel pot and let stand for three hours. Then bring to a boil and simmer until thick, about one hour. Seal in hot sterilized jars. Yield: Six to seven half-pints.

Author's guarantee: If you eat enough of these fig preserves, you will soon be writing like Eudora Welty! I guarantee it.

∼A native of Alabama, Wade Hall has lived since 1962 in Louisville, Kentucky, where he has taught English and chaired the English and Humanities programs at Kentucky Southern College and Bellarmine College. He has also taught at the University of Florida. He holds degrees from Troy State University, the University of Alabama, and the University of Illinois. For fifteen years he edited *The Kentucky Poetry Review*. He is the author of books, monographs, articles, plays, and reviews relating to Kentucky and southern history and literature. His most recent books include *Sacred Violance: A Reader's Companion to Cormac McCarthy*, *Complete Conviction: The Private Life of Wilson W. Wyatt, Sr.*; *Hell-Bent for Music: The Life of Pee Wee King;* and *A Visit with Harlan Hubbard.*

The Tao of Cornbread

RONNI LUNDY

"There are those who will tell you that real cornbread has just a little sugar in it. They'll say it enhances the flavor or that it's an old tradition in the South. Do not listen to them. If God had meant for cornbread to have sugar in it, he'd have called it cake."

These words began an article I wrote for *Esquire* magazine some fifteen years ago on the art of making real cornbread. A recipe for cornbread forms the heart of the piece, and in order to write that recipe out in cups and teaspoons, I had to go back and systematically take apart something I had been doing and taking for granted most of my life.

I learned to make cornbread standing next to my mother in the kitchen. I don't know that she has ever used a measuring spoon or cup—certainly not for something as fundamental as our daily pan of cornbread. What she did was mix the basic ingredients together in a bowl until everything looked right. If you asked her how much of something she used to do this, her answer would be "enough." To find out how much was "enough" in cups and tablespoons, I had to dump cornmeal into a mixing bowl until it "looked right," then dump it back into a measuring cup, then level it off to the nearest even amount. I had to pour milk from a measuring cup until the batter "looked right," then go back and calculate how much was gone. By the time I was finished, I thought I'd earned a degree in chemistry.

And after I'd calculated exactly how to make the recipe, I also had to tell folks why it is they'd want to go to the trouble. I had to explain the rare magic of this simple food, explain how come such a seemingly ordinary thing could turn any meal at which it appears into a special eating event. I had to think about the qualities of cornbread afresh. As I did, I began to appreciate the fierce and even heat of the skillet, which gives the bread its distinctive crust—and to understand how it's the contrast of the crisp, dark crust with the smooth, creamy interior, or the subtle sweetness of the corn playing off against the sharp tang of the drippings, that gives cornbread its life. Cornbread is a lot like culture.

I was born in Corbin, Kentucky, the daughter of Pap and Jerry Lundy. And whenever my parents talked about "going up home," Corbin is what they meant. But when I was one year old, my daddy had the offer of a job in Louisville, so he borrowed an old panel truck and packed all of our belongings in it. He put the divan across the back of that truck, and my mother says that's how she and I rode to Louisville, her sitting on that divan holding me in her arms and the two of us crying all the way.

But I don't cry now when I think back upon my childhood. We were poor people, but those were in many ways the richest of times. We moved first to an apartment over on Oak Street where it runs into 18th, or the Dixie Highway. And then when I was seven years old, my sister, Pat, who was a teenager at the time, found a home for sale on Third Street where it runs into Southern Parkway, and I lived there until I went away to college. Those homes I grew up in were bustling and exciting places, busy as train depots. And they were junctions of a sort—stations on the underground railroad of the hillbilly diaspora of the 1950s and early 60s.

A diaspora, of course, is any time that a group of people are exiled from their homeland by an outside force. That force can be an act of nature, like an earthquake, or it can be a man-made force such as war or famine or poverty. In our case, it was poverty that forced us to leave the foothills of the Cumberland Mountains, which we loved. And maybe that's why I always have such a hard time remembering the correct way to pronounce diaspora. Instead of accenting that second syllable, I always want to put the stress on the first, saying, "die-us-poor-uh," which, my friend Shirley Williams has pointed out, sounds exactly like "Die as poor as a hillbilly. . ." which is what we were all going to do if we didn't get out of there.

So, like my parents, our cousins, kin, and friends were leaving home for the offer of jobs somewhere else, almost always somewhere "up north." On the way to places such as Detroit, Chicago, Dayton, and Hamilton, Ohio, our house was the place they stopped to refuel and replenish. They'd sit around this big round oak table we had in the dining room and for hours they'd tell stories with my daddy. And they'd stoke up on my mother's good home cooking: fried chicken and shuck beans, killed lettuce (only we called it "wilted" when company was there), okra succotash, slumgullion, and, at every meal, unless we were having biscuits, a fresh hot skillet of cornbread.

I was nourished at that table on far more than good food. The people who sat around it were an ever-entertaining, ever-fascinating circle of friends and mentors who brought constant surprise and delight to my childhood. One time it was my cousin Betty Jean in the place of honor, and she had arrived bearing a Betty Crocker bake set just for me—a perk from her husband Jack's new job with General Mills. Another season it was my cousin, David, who lived in Japan and wrote books and stories for the *New Yorker*. And sometimes it was my glamorous cousin, Faye, who had found the best job of anybody in the diaspora, singing in front of the Don Pablo orchestra in Detroit: a gig that meant she got to wear tight dresses with puffy sleeves and hats with fruit cascading down the brim.

For a while we had a fellow living with us named Bill Moore who taught me how to play cards. He might have been a distant cousin, and for sure he had been an old sparring partner of my dad's. He had also been a sailor and wore a blue cap and had a squinched up eye and gimpy leg, so I thought that Popeye the sailor man had come to live with us.

My great-aunt Minnie came to live with us for a while after my Uncle Finley died, and although that was a sad occasion, I was secretly happy because Aunt Minnie was a wonderful friend to have in the house if you were a child. She could sew—a skill which no one in my immediate family ever mastered—and when she made clothes for me, she'd always buy a little extra material to make a matching outfit for my doll. She also made the best fried apple pies, and just before I'd be getting home from school on a winter day, she'd fry one up so when I opened the back door into the kitchen I'd be greeted with the smell of tangy apples steeped in brown sugar and the buttery crust of that pie.

Every house my mother has ever lived in has had more beds in it than there were people actually living in the house, and when I was a child those beds were filled with an ever-changing, ever-interesting cast of characters. There were cousins my age who would suddenly be there staying with us while their folks looked for a new job or house. And we'd be thick as thieves and close as siblings for a few days and then, just about the time we'd start to get sick of one another, they'd be moving on. And there were the distinguished aunts on daddy's side of the family who came to town on the L&N railroad, wearing their mink stoles with the dead animal heads flapping on the sides. And whenever they arrived I'd be really excited because I knew that meant that later on that evening we'd all pile into cars and cabs and head off to downtown Louisville for an elegant dinner—at the Blue Boar Cafeteria.

Most of the meals we had when company came were consumed around the round oak table, though. And it was around that table that I learned the lessons of my life, the stories that told me who I was and where I came from, the stories that led me to imagine where I might go. It was around that table that I heard about my mother's almost idyllic childhood in Corbin and heard the rambunctious tales of my daddy's young manhood working in the three Cs (Civilian Conservation Corps) in the Cumberland Valley. It was around that table that I learned what my grandparents were like. All four of them were dead long before I was born, but because of the stories told around that table, I felt as if I'd grown up with them all, conscious and present in my life as if they'd actually been there. I took those stories in greedily, hungrily, and was nourished on them like they were a glass of cold sweet milk and a wedge of my mother's golden, steaming fresh cornbread.

Now, when I grew up and moved away from my childhood home, started making my own life, my own daily pan of cornbread, I discovered that many of my peers had not grown up at all as I had. They had lived in neat suburban homes that housed only one nuclear family, their dinners were made of frozen foods and Big Macs, their entertainment and instruction in life were provided by a television set. There were elements of these things in my growing up, too—after all, I was a child of the '50s and '60s. But I had also been fed on big steaming bowls of soup beans and cornbread, had learned my lessons from the likes of Bill Moore and Aunt Minnie.

I soon discovered, though, that no matter how much I valued these things, when I told my friends about them, they could only hear my stories as either slightly perverse or rustically hilarious—extensions of the hillbilly fantasies they'd been fed by *Deliverance* or the *Beverly Hillbillies.* And it became important to me to learn how to tell these stories to my friends with the same weight, the same nuances and meaning, that they had for me. To do that, I was compelled to go back and define my hillbilly roots for myself. And just as I'd done with that recipe for cornbread, I found I had to take a fresh look at something I'd taken for granted all my life. I found that I had to take it all apart and put it back together again in order to know what it was really about.

The first step was easy. That was to reclaim all the good traits that others denied me. What does it mean to be a hillbilly? I asked. Well, it meant having a quick wit and ingenuity—enough to reach up in the sky and down into the river and grab electricity the way my friend Shirley's uncle had done with his wind- and water-powered generators up in Dwarf, Kentucky. It meant coming from people who had a love of storytelling—not just a fascination with plot and character, but a passion for the rhythm and music of the language as it rolls off the tongue. It meant coming from people who cling fiercely to independence, not only their own, but that of every person; and it meant coming from a people who will respect others for what they are, not for where they came from or what they own. It meant being raised by people with a spirit of generosity so deep it would open the door and give food and shelter not only to family and friends, but to needy strangers: making a pallet on the floor, if need be, and slicing the pan of cornbread into as many pieces as it takes to make sure everyone at the table is fed. It meant coming from a people whose love for their children and their elders is deep enough to reach from beyond the grave and touch the heart. It meant being from a culture that makes great music and useful tools and that can create delicious, nourishing food from mean and meager stores. I said, "These are mine. And they are good and fine and I am proud of them. That's part of who I am and where I come from."

The next step was harder. That was to claim the darkness. The sad truth is that in every stereotype there lies a kernel of truth—that is what makes it so powerful. So I had to look that truth square in the face and acknowledge that everything about the culture I came from wasn't a cause for joy. I had to acknowledge the violence and blood feuds that have stained the mountains my family came from. I had to accept the destruction of the land and the meanness of spirit that have also marred the heritage that I claim. I had to accept the bitterness of sometimes-cold religions that can shut a person out or even break a family apart. I had to acknowledge that this was a culture that sometimes held women in a low and despised place, and in which men have allowed drink to ruin them and those around them.

These, too, are a part of my roots—and I needed to acknowledge them. I couldn't have the real recipe for my culture, I couldn't get the full flavor of what made me, until I put them in the pan along with the good things. It was like that cornbread, like the crust contrasted to the creamy center, the tang to the sweetness, the dark to the light. Unless you have them both, you can't have the whole. Unless you have the shadows, you can't really discern the light. Unless you have the bitter, you won't really taste the sweet. And it's all these things together, the way they play off against one another, that create something whole that is special and wonderful and rare.

Now, if you want to make a pan of real cornbread, here's what you do. First get a good cast-iron skillet. An old, well-seasoned and well-used one is best. It may look greasy and caked-up on the outside, but that just means you'll get a better crust. Into this pan goes a big spoonful of drippings. Butter is good, but bacon grease is best—gritted with tiny flecks of the meat and redolent with its tangy savor.

Put the skillet in an oven where the fire is already white-hot and scorching—about 450 degrees.

Dump some cornmeal—about two cups' worth—in a big bowl. Mountain people prefer white cornmeal because it's got a sharper taste and tenderer texture. Put in some salt for savor, and a little baking soda and baking powder for just a little rise, but not too much. Remember, real cornbread is never puffed-up or self-important.

Crack a big egg in the middle and break it with your wooden spoon. Add milk—about a cup-and-a-half worth. Sweet milk is just fine, but if you've got buttermilk, you've got good eating.

Stir it up and about then your drippings should be good and hot. Take your skillet out of the oven and swirl it to coat it. It should crackle and pop like the laughter of your cousins when your daddy just told a good one.

Pour the grease into the batter, mix it in quick, pour the batter back into the skillet, and pop it into the oven. Now here's the hard part. You're going to have to wait for twenty to twenty-five minutes. And while you're waiting you're going to start to smell that sweet, buttery scent of the corn, the seductive saltiness of the bacon grease. And when you pull that skillet out of the oven, the cornbread will have a golden-brown glistening crust that will crack crisply as you make that first slice. And when you pull that first wedge up out of the pan, a little cloud of corn-sweet steam will rise up in your face.

And, buddy, that will be the best food you'll ever eat in your life.

⌒Ronni Lundy's interest in food began only moments after she was born in Corbin, Kentucky, in 1949. Professionally, this interest has resulted in two cookbooks, *The Festive Table*, (Northpoint Press, 1995) and *Shuck Beans, Stack Cakes and Honest Fried Chicken*, (Atlantic Monthly Press, 1991) with a third, *Butterbeans to Blackberries,* due in 1998. Her articles on food have appeared in numerous publications from *Esquire* to *Historic Preservation* magazines, and the *Louisville Courier-Journal* to the *Cleveland Plain-Dealer*. Her treatise on the art of making Real Cornbread, originally published in *Esquire*, has been reprinted in four college textbooks. Lundi is the former editor of *Louisville* magazine, and before that she was the author of a monthly column there that was nominated for a James Beard award in 1994. Lundy was a judge for the IACP's Julia Child awards from 1993-95. Previously, Lundy spent twelve years as a feature writer for *The Courier-Journal* and *Louisville Times* and was both pop music critic and the restaurant reviewer. She has lived in Santa Fe, Santa Barbara, Colorado, Maine, and Baltimore and worked in dozens of restaurants before realizing that writing was a much more sedentary career. She currently resides in Louisville, Kentucky, and has a remarkably brilliant daughter, a notably charming spouse, and a most excellent 1954 Kenmore gas range.

Just Add Words

GEORGE ELLA LYON

People often ask if there have been other writers in my family. Until I began digging through my grandmother's recipes, my answer was, "Lots of storytellers, but only two writers: my father, who kept a journal, and my brother, who writes literary criticism." But sifting through my culinary inheritance has broadened my response, just as all the recipes' butter and bacon grease have broadened the rest of me.

When my daddy's mother, Josephine Wilder Hoskins, died in 1985, I inherited her recipes, I who am what became of the little girl who sat at her table. Jo left a few cookbooks not much used—*Better Homes and Gardens, The Harlan Woman's Club Silver Anniversary Collection*—and a 1964

Yearbook, provided by the local insurance company, with recipes pasted in or stuck between the pages. Most of these recipes came from newspapers—the *Harlan Daily Enterprise*, the *Knoxville News Sentinel*, the *St. Petersburg Times*—but some were clipped from magazines, cut from cornstarch and cracker boxes, or written on a variety of papers in a variety of hands. For me, this once-white, plastic-coated-cardboard, double-ring-bound book is magic. Leafing through it leads me back to my grandmother's four-room apartment, to her walnut dining table and her shiny black kitchen table, to the taste of my grandmother's life.

Jo hated to keep house, though (or perhaps because) she did it meticulously, but she loved to cook. Cook and fuss. Get something bubbling on each cap of the stove—she called them *caps* long after the woodstove was gone—and worry that food till it was done. Swiss steak, tender as a kiss, swimming in tomatoes and peppers. A kettle of pinto beans, rich with the sweetness of streaked meat. A big pot of vegetable soup with everything you'd hope for and then turnips. Potatoes boiling, soon to be mashed, with little butter lakes in between the peaks. And best of all, best of anything she might make, even desserts: a cast-iron skillet brimming with fried corn.

Jo fried corn at least once a week as long as corn was in season. Going through her recipes I discovered they fell into three equal categories: Dessert, Corn, and Neither Dessert nor Corn. (That's only a slight exaggeration.) Dessert did not surprise me, since Jo was famous for her butterscotch and chocolate pies, jam cake with caramel icing, fudge, and sea foam candy. The cookie jar at her house was never empty, and it was she who once declared, "Every tooth in my head is a sweet tooth!"

But *corn*? The only way she fixed corn as far as I knew was *fried*, and she sure didn't need a recipe for that. She had them, though: fried corn, creamed corn, corn pudding, corn and vienna sausage casserole, mexicorn, corn fritters, gritted corn, cornpone pie. Corn relish, baby-corn pickles, corn chowder, succotash. Everything but the mountain delicacy I conjured to my soon-to-be husband: corn cut whole from the cob, each kernel stuffed with beads of seasoned hamburger and sewn back on with corn silks. I told Steve I grew up on this dish. He almost believed me till I got to the corn silks. Always resist that last detail.

But why did my grandmother have this obsession with corn? In my memory, she cooked a lot more beef than corn; why not a wad of recipes for steak and roast and hamburger?

I think the answer lies in the fields of the little farm her daddy had on Brownie's Creek, in the corn she hoed and shucked and shelled and gritted, in the fodder shocks she hid behind and the cobs she played with. Corn figured in some major stories of her life: the one time she took a drink of moonshine distilled corn—and her eyes swelled shut so that her sister "shied cobs at [her] the whole morning"; my grandfather's letter proposing marriage and promising, "You'll never have to hoe corn again," and her elopement, by buggy, straight from the cornfield.

Her roots were in corn, and in it, too, was some of the paradox of her life. We think of corn as plain food, plain enough to share with livestock—field corn, of course, not sweet corn—but the plant itself is extravagant, with its ribbony leaves and its tasseled fruit so strangely upholstered, apocryphal. Jo, likewise, was a hill farm girl determined to be a city woman. She left the fields and was dressed up ever after, refusing even to grow a house plant. No ties to the land for her. *Fine things* were what she wanted: clothes, jewelry, furniture.

And sometimes even the furniture tied her down too much. Two years before I was born she decided she didn't want a house at all. She wanted to live in the Llewelyn Hotel. Ever obliging, Papaw sold the house and they moved. It got old, though, living in such cramped quarters, eating only what someone else decided to fix. Who knows, maybe they didn't serve enough corn. Anyway, after a year Papaw built an apartment house, and they moved into the rooms where they would live the rest of their lives.

Jo's father died soon after, and her trips home to the creek became rare. But in her last years, as present time gave way, the farm came back to her. When my father had surgery and I called from the hospital to say it had gone well, Jo apologized for not making the long trip to Knoxville with us, saying, "You know I wanted to come, but I had to stay here and take care of these horses. A farm's a thing you can't walk off and leave." Standing at the hospital pay phone, I pictured her talking to me from her little apartment bedroom. Did she think the stable was in the kitchen? Did the horses of her memory browse at the dining room table?

Leaving the farm had been a major accomplishment in her life, yet all those years in town she went on cooking corn, just as they had down on the creek, for summer feasts and winter survival. Corn must have fed something deep, and she wanted to have plenty of ways to fix it. Perhaps she laid up recipes the way her family put up the corn itself.

Jo always said the best recipe for corn was, "Boil the water while you go to the field," but since that wasn't an option in town she settled for frying it.

Fried corn is a little more complicated. As is often the case with Jo's recipes, this one has no measurements. You're supposed to know how the result should look and just taste and add ingredients till you get there. This is easier for a stove-top dish like corn than for some of her cakes, the directions for which say, in woodstove fashion, "Bake in hot oven until done."

Once you have your corn—preferably from your garden, a farmer's market, or a truck by the side of the road, you have to cut it from the cob in three steps. This is crucial. If you just whack those kernels off in one try, like Jack the Giant Killer whacking off heads, you might as well go to the Green Giant for your corn. No, working with a bowl rather than a board, you have to cut about halfway through the kernel on the first slice so that plenty of sweet juice is freed for taste and texture. Then you clip down through the remaining kernel and then you scrape the cob—close, close—like a young man shaving his chin.

Besides the freshest corn possible, the foundation ingredient of fried corn is bacon grease. Melt that with some butter in your big black skillet and spoon in the milky corn. You'll be adding some cream and salt and pepper to this as it simmers and you'll want to taste often to check on the flavor and to hold you over till mealtime. The whole project, what with shucking, silking, cutting, scraping, and simmering, will take about two hours. It's not quick, but quicker than writing this essay, and the taste is beyond compare.

One day, when I was sifting through Jo's book, the edge of a pasted-in recipe came loose and I peeled it off. Underneath was my grandfather's handwriting! *Wed. morning, 5" snow. I ordered 2 bedspreads from Sears Roebuck Co., Greensboro, N.C. Cleaning out air restart Box at Bowling Building*, it said. Quickly I found another loose recipe and peeled it away. *Went to Sunday School and Church and night service. Went to see J. P. McPheron. Robert Hoskins 3 called from school at 9 o'clock tonight.* The words swam in front of me. Papaw, who quit school after fourth grade to work the farm, had been using the insurance company yearbook as a journal! I never knew he wrote anything. Alongside this revelation was the fact that Jo, who quit school in seventh grade because she "was getting so big [she] was afraid they'd make [her] the teacher," had papered over his words. What did this mean, that she pasted food over thought, her responsibility over his reflection?

Ten years ago, I would have had a lot to say about this, but now I know I don't know. It's too much for me, a mystery as deep as streamers of corn leaves unfurling from dry seed you held in your hand. All I can do is handle the news carefully, a tender artifact, like the recipes I find written on checks from different banks, the ones on a ticket from my father's dry cleaners, a radio station memo pad, and the back of a Soul-Winning Visitation Card from the Baptist Women's Missionary Union.

Directions for making Cranberry Sparkle fill the back of page two of a letter, which picks up mid-sentence:

for the cold winter days
am glad Bertha is
looking much better
she sure had room for
improvement.

Then there is one in pencil on notebook paper in what looks like my other grandmother's hand: The heading is just "Bourbon," but the recipe is for that holiday confection called Bourbon Balls. It ends, "Keep cool until ready to serve, and will they vanish!"

Since, like Bertha, we all have room for improvement, and since we all, sweet or not, will vanish, I'll refrain from judging my grandmother. For all I know, she may have asked my grandfather if she could use the yearbook and he may have said, "Go right ahead." So I'll just add Papaw to the list of family writers. I'll fry corn each summer, the way Jo taught me, and pass the recipe and the story on to you.

ᘒBorn and raised in the mountains of Kentucky, George Ella Lyon grew up with a love of poetry and music. She graduated from Centre College with a B.A., from University of Arkansas with an M.A., and from Indiana University with a Ph.D., all in English. Lyon now lives in Lexington, Kentucky, with her husband and two sons. She has published two collections of poems (*Mountain* and *Catalpa*, winner of the Appalachian Book of the Year award), fourteen picture books (including *Come a Tide*, featured on *Reading Rainbow*; *Who Came Down That Road?*, a *Publishers' Weekly* Best Book of the Year; and *Basket*, winner of the Kentucky Bluegrass Award), three novels for young readers (including *Borrowed Children*, winner of the Golden Kite Award), an autobiography (*A Wordful Child*, in the Richard Owen Meet-the-Author series), and *Choices*, a book of stories for adult new readers. Her work is featured in the new PBS series, *The United States of Poetry*.

Grandma Jess's Easy East Rolls

ED MCCLANAHAN

My mother—Grandma Jess, my kids called her—died on August 29, 1996. She was eighty-eight, happy and healthy, living independently among friends and family, still driving her own car, still enjoying a Bloody Mary every Saturday before lunch, when, while she was watching her beloved Democrats on TV one evening during the convention, she dropped off to sleep and never woke up. She was a beautiful, warm, vivacious woman, and we all miss her powerfully. But she left a splendid legacy of good will and good humor, generosity of spirit, all-encompassing affection . . . and the priceless recipe for her incomparable "east" rolls.

My mother, bless her heart, was given to creative pronunciation. After my folks sent me to Europe in 1953, she couldn't get enough of my accounts of an Alpine fantasy she called "Switcherland." Born Jessie Poage, she became a McClanahan twice over—long after my father's death she married his brother, making her Jess McClanahan McClanahan—yet for more than sixty years she called herself, "Jess McClanniehan." She was an avid horsewoman, and for many years she kept a handsome Tennessee walking "harse" named Tonto. And, bearing the latter articulation in mind, you can readily imagine that what she did to that number that comes after thirty-nine was positively scandalous.

That brings us to her fabled east rolls, a primary ingredient of which is—you guessed it—yeast.

During most of my childhood and adolescence in Brooksville (the seat of government, commerce, and culture in all of Bracken County, as everybody knows), we lived two doors from the Methodist church and next door to the Methodist parsonage. The proximity required that, although my parents were not notably religious (nor irreligious, for that matter, despite my dad's fondness for bourbon, tobacco, poker, and the ponies), we went to Sunday school and church every Sunday—religiously, as it were. Afterwards, to reward our piety, we treated ourselves to a sumptuous family Sunday dinner. I was an only child, so my immediate family was on the smallish side, but there were always enough aunts, uncles, grannies, and other company to guarantee a groaning board.

The standard entree of those Sunday dinners was a pot roast the size of the crankcase of a Massey-Ferguson tractor, ringed like Saturn by a garland of potatoes, carrots, brussels sprouts, and onions. There was also a "relish tray"—radishes, celery, raw carrots, green onions, olives, pickles, and similar low-priority comestibles—, a couple of side dishes, green beans, say, cooked to a fare-thee-well (*Al Dente*? Who the hell is *Al Dente*?), a corn pudding so creamy and sweet it would break your heart, a gravy boat brimful *of l'essence d'un pot de boeuf* (or, as I once heard a waitress in a Mississippi cafe call it, "aw juice"), and the vessel which, in point of fact, preceded the gravy boat in its stately voyage around the table, a breadbasket filled to the gunnels with those plump, toothsome, golden-brown dinner rolls, piping hot beneath a starched white linen napkin.

But before the breadbasket and the gravy boat could dock at my plate (block that metaphor!), I had one onerous duty to perform: The Blessing.

To my chagrin, my status as resident Cute Kid had automatically anointed me the designated grace-sayer; so back when I was five or six years old, several of my aunts had ganged up on me and made me memorize some perfunctory little rhyming pietism on the order of "Good bread, good meat! / Good God, let's eat!" which I dutifully rattled off before every Sunday dinner. With the impending feast literally right under my nose, however, concentration was often hard to maintain, and I sometimes conferred my blessing so peremptorily that I forgot altogether what I was supposed to be saying: One Sunday, in place of my usual high-speed incantation, I heard myself solemnly intoning the Lord's Prayer; another time, the Pledge of Allegiance.

But the next thing I knew, all that would somehow be behind me, whereas *before* me was a dinner plate featuring pot roast with its supporting cast of vegetables, and there beside it would be that basket of rolls, all steamy and savory when you broke them open and exposed their soft, snow-white interiors. And the gravy boat was a-comin'; its sails were in sight!

The rolls came in two styles; some opened into two sections, some into three. The two-section ones were best for cold roast beef sandwiches at Sunday evening dinner—so I passed those over (and crossed my fingers that everyone else would do the same) in favor of the three-section variety, which provided more interior surfaces for soaking up the aw juice. For the same reason, they were also best for buttering, so when the basket came my way I always helped myself to three of them, two for gravy and the third for that even more exalted purpose. And when the butter had melted—and my mother wasn't looking—I'd sprinkle sugar on the buttered sides, for a sort of preliminary mid-dinner dessert, to ready my palate for the pie or cake or custard or cobbler I knew would shortly be forthcoming.

My interest in the culinary arts has always pretty much been confined to the finished product (though I can whip up a pretty fair dry martini, when I have to), but the genesis of the yeast rolls caught my imagination like the Petty Girls in my dad's monthly *Esquire*.

Sunday's rolls began their brief but glorious lives on Saturday night, when my mom mixed up a batch of gray, flaccid, lumpy, singularly unpromising-looking glop in a big bowl, covered it with a damp dishtowel, and stashed it in the fridge, where it languished until after church the next morning, by which time it had somehow ballooned to twice its original size and become this smooth, pale orb that seemed almost to glow with its own inner light, like a little moon caught in a mixing bowl—or, come to think of it, like a Petty Girl.

But I digress.

My wife, Hilda (speaking of Petty Girls), is the only cook I've ever known who belonged in the same kitchen with my mother. Hilda's from Belgium, and—poor ignorant, benighted, unsophisticated European that she is—for the longest time she thought that "east rolls" came from the east, or were special Easter treats or something. Fortunately for the future of civilization, however, she inherited my mother's recipe, and with it the mantle of reigning East Roll Queen of the Known World.

I've named them "Grandma Jess's *Easy* East Rolls," by the way, because when Hilda asked her how to make them, she declared, characteristically, "Oh honey, they're just *real* easy!" Nonetheless, it took Hilda four tries to get them right. The lessons she learned from her first three attempts, Hilda says, are: be sure you use cake yeast, not powdered, be sure the yeast is fresh, and be sure the oven is plenty hot (425 degrees).

Well hey, enough idle chit-chat. Good God, let's eat!

Grandma Jess's Easy East Rolls

one-half cup warm water (plus or minus 110 degrees)
one cake yeast
three tablespoons Crisco
three tablespoons sugar
one teaspoon salt
one cup hot (not boiling) milk
four cups all-purpose flour

Dissolve yeast in warm water. In a separate bowl, combine Crisco, sugar, and salt. Pour hot milk over these and stir until Crisco is melted. When this mixture is lukewarm, pour yeast mixture over it and mix everything together. Add four cups of flour, one at a time, kneading until it makes a soft dough. (If still sticky, add a little more flour). Put dough in a greased bowl, cover bowl with foil or a damp cloth, and refrigerate overnight (or until dough has doubled). Punch down the dough, roll it out, and cut with biscuit-cutter. Divide each "biscuit" into three (or, for two-section rolls, two) equal-sized pieces, roll into little balls, and place in greased muffin tin. Let rise again (at room temperature) for about twenty minutes, meanwhile pre-heating oven to 425 degrees. Bake for fifteen minutes.

～Ed McClanahan is a native of northeastern Kentucky; he was born in Brooksville in 1932, and grew up there and in Maysville, where he graduated from high school in 1951. He attended Miami University (A.B., 1955) and the University of Kentucky (M.A., 1958), and has taught English and creative writing at Oregon State University, Stanford University, the University of Montana, the University of Kentucky, and Northern Kentucky University. His books include *The Natural Man* (a novel), *Famous People I Have Known* (a serio-comic autobiography), and *A Congress Of Wonders* (three novellas). His work has appeared in many magazines, including *Esquire*, *Rolling Stone*, and *Playboy*, and twice won *Playboy's* Best Nonfiction awards. He has also been awarded a Wallace Stegner Fellowship in Creative Writing at Stanford, two Yaddo Fellowships, and an Al Smith Fellowship. He lives with his wife, Hilda, in Lexington, Kentucky, where (with the help of his friend and collaborator Tom Marksbury) he is assembling a volume of previously uncollected "McClanahaniana" titled *My Vita, If You Will*. He is also "thinking about" a new novel, a latter-day sequel to *The Natural Man*, titled "Return of the Son of Needmore."

Slices

MAUREEN MOREHEAD

Bread

Ellen Spurlock was born on Moore Creek in eastern Kentucky in 1911 in a one-room cabin with a dirt floor. She lived there until she was twelve, then moved to Flat Lick, attended school until she was sixteen, then rode her father's mule to a one-room schoolhouse on Mill Branch where she taught first through twelfth grades until the doctor's son, Nevil Morehead, on his way to law school in Louisville, married her and took her there.

Nevil and Ellen lived in a four-room house on Larchmont Avenue until he died in 1956 at forty-five of a massive heart attack, leaving Ellen to raise four children, Doris, Janice, James, and the youngest, Robert, whom I married in 1974.

To take care of her family, Ellen learned to drive, then got a job teaching. Eventually, she earned a bachelor's degree. She retired from the Jefferson County Public Schools in 1981.

My mother-in-law is eighty-five. She still lives in the white, aluminum-sided house on Larchmont. The odd thing about the house is that it faces the house two doors down, which faces it, rather than the street. Why? She cannot tell me.

Every Derby Day about a thousand buses roll down Larchmont, shuttling out-of-towners to Churchill Downs. Ellen calls us, and we can hear engines in the background.

Twice a week, my husband's mother bakes sourdough bread, six loaves, two each for her three children who still live in Louisville. Sometimes she gets in her 1987 gray Honda Accord and delivers the sweet loaves to her family. Other times, her children, all teachers, stop by the house to visit their mother and pick them up. Sometimes I say we don't need so much bread, but Janice reminds me that kneading is good for Ellen's rheumatism.

On Saturday mornings, Robert or I make French toast for each other and our son, Clint, using his mother's sourdough bread. (Stir eggs, brown sugar, milk, and cinnamon in a bowl, dip in the bread, and fry in a skillet in which you've melted a little butter.) The truth is, we've never had better breakfasts, even when we were children.

Potions

I got in trouble once when I thought it would be funny to add a bottle of Hershey's syrup and a jar of dill pickles to the spaghetti sauce we Chi Omega pledges were making for our future sorority sisters. We thought it was a good joke, but they didn't laugh, claiming we'd ruined the dinner they'd planned for some special guests, probably their boyfriends or some really important alumnae.

At eighteen, I was a little old to be playing with food, but my inability to take it too seriously extends back to my childhood.

It was 1978, Jacksonville, Illinois, and my best friend, Kathy Watson, and I formed the DDTT Club, the two purposes of which were to ostracize our sisters and to make horrible potions (the second a useful way to accomplish the first, as we required our sisters to taste the potions to join the club).

DDTT stood for "double double toil and trouble." Where I heard the Shakespeare, I don't remember, but Kathy and I assumed the witches' roles, stirring various "natural ingredients"—grass, rocks, dandelions, buckeyes, wild violets, crabapples, black walnuts, and, best of all, because it smelled so bad and curdled, milk—into quart-sized mayonnaise jars, which we arranged by the color of their contents on the shelves in our storageroom-in-the-garage clubhouse.

This stuff we made was sickening, and, at some point, Kathy and I realized it, so one morning I dumped every batch into a ditch that ran between our families' backyards.

Neither Kathy nor I grew up in Jacksonville. My father decided to become a teacher and moved our family to Kentucky; Mr. Watson's company, soon afterwards, transferred him to Texas. I've often wondered where Kathy is now and what she's doing. Is she a chemist? Does she bake? I'm not, and I don't. Nor am I a Chi Omega alumna.

Bologna

I know this is dangerous, but if you want a really good bologna sandwich for lunch, make it the night before, put on a lot of mayonnaise, then let it sit in a brown paper sack in a dark locker in an elementary school for as long as it takes to do spelling, arithmetic, and gym, then eat it in a big cafeteria with walls the color of pistachio pudding. Trust me. That bologna sandwich will take you back thirty-five years.

Grandma Mahoney didn't come to visit often. She lived in Buffalo, New York, on Chateau Terrace in a two-story white house with a huge front yard. A cherry tree grew outside her kitchen window. In that kitchen, because I got up at six a.m. with my grandmother, I first tasted sweet, creamy coffee and ate strawberry shortcake for breakfast.

My mother would not have approved had she known I was eating dessert for breakfast. Unhealthy, she'd say, plus you'd better watch what you put in your mouth, young lady, or you'll look like that big, fat lady ahead of us walking up the steps into church or standing in the checkout lane at the A&P.

My mother was right. I was a pudgy eight-year-old and have always had to watch my weight. But, whereas my mother couldn't understand how a kindergartner could add a layer of saltine crackers to her bologna sandwich one summer day (when Grandma was visiting), thereby swallowing her first loose tooth, thereby having nothing to leave under her pillow for the tooth fairy, my grandmother did understand. For she was a very large woman with a very big heart.

Cookies

There's not much of a story behind my grandmother Jostes's black walnut cookies except that they are my grandmother's recipe and that my father loved and misses her.

By the time I was old enough to remember her, my small, stoic, German grandmother had been married to her second husband, Arch Jostes, for a long time. Her first husband, William Podshadley, my grandfather, was a mechanic. He was killed by a drunk driver as he changed a tire for a stranded motorist on Christmas Day, 1941, when my father was thirteen. After the accident, my grandmother moved my father, his two older sisters, and one younger brother from Farmersville, Illinois, to Springfield so that she could find work and take care of her family.

Sometime later, when the kids were raised, Louise married Arch, and we saw them twice a year, on Thanksgiving in Springfield, where they lived; and on Christmas, in Jacksonville, thirty miles away, where my father, after dental school and a stint in the Air Force, eventually settled for a while to raise his five daughters.

The first thing you had to do when you got to Grandma and Arch's house for the holiday was to kiss and be kissed by them. Kissing Arch was creepy, Grandma Jostes's kisses perfunctory—but not her Thanksgiving dinners. On the big dining room table covered with a white lace cloth were creamed corn, green beans, peas, fried okra, mashed potatoes, candied sweet potatoes, rhubarb, cranberry sauce, sliced ham, roast turkey, sweet-raisin dressing, all spooned into pink and green Depression glass bowls or laid out on white china platters, and in the kitchen on the little yellow metal table, the pies: peach, pumpkin, gooseberry, and mincemeat. And the black walnut cookies.

Here's what I remember about my grandmother Jostes's house: It was big and white and sat on a quiet street lined with elm trees. My grandmother and Arch owned the house, but lived in the second floor apartment; Mary and Dick lived in the apartment below them. Outside Mary's front window was a white wooden porch swing. We kids had to be quiet when we played on it. The couch in the living room was pink and scratchy;

a TV stood in a corner in that room, but we seldom watched it. African violets bloomed in the kitchen, dining room, and living room windows, and though my grandmother often gave leaves to my mother so that she too could have the pretty flowers, they never survived the darker rooms of our house in Jacksonville. In the bedroom where we slept when we stayed overnight, the ceiling was high, the furniture mahogany, the wood-work dark, the walls papered in big red flowers, and on the walls were pictures of Jesus holding his bleeding heart and William and Louise, young and severe, just minutes after their 1921 marriage. To get to the cellar, you opened an awkward wooden door attached to the back of the house. Inside was a cool, damp space and the washing machine. To get to the attic, you climbed a flight of narrow stairs just off the sunroom where we kids ate our Thanksgiving dinner. Once, when just my grandmother and I were up there, she gave me a blue-speckled coffeepot, a wedding gift to her and William, and her father's German Bible.

The year she died of a heart attack, 1985 (my father has had three), I baked my grandmother Jostes's black walnut cookies for Christmas for my father. It is the best gift, he tells me periodically, I ever gave him.

Black Walnut Cookies

two cups sugar
one cup margarine
three eggs
one cup sour milk (may be made by adding one teaspoon vinegar to one
    cup milk)
four cups flour
one teaspoon baking soda
one teaspoon cinnamon
three-fourths teaspoon cloves
one cup chopped black walnuts
one cup dates or raisins

Preheat oven to 350 degrees. Mix sour milk and soda. Cream sugar and butter, add eggs, then milk and soda mixture. Add spices and flour, nuts and fruit. Drop by the spoonful onto a greased baking sheet and bake until slightly brown on top.

∽Maureen Morehead is a poet, wife, mother, and schoolteacher. She has published many poems in such journals as *The American Poetry Review*, *The Iowa Review*, *The California Quarterly*, *The Southern Poetry Review*, *The Black Warrior Review*, and *The Louisville Review*. She has also published two books,

In a Yellow Room and, with Pat Carr, *Our Brothers' War* (The Sulgrave Press), and has received grants from the Kentucky Arts Council and the Kentucky Foundation for Women for her poetry. She has a Ph.D. in English from the University of Louisville and teaches English, journalism, and creative writing at duPont Manual High School in Louisville, Kentucky, where she also advises the school newspaper and the literary magazine.

Of Reading, Writing, and Recipes: Sunshine Cake

SENA JETER NASLUND

Each with a round face, we three seem to look out innocently, from our station on the mantel, at those people we are becoming over the years. In the hand-tinted photograph, John, four, and Marvin, six, are wearing shorts and T-shirts, and Marvin's shirt has an applique of a small airplane, circa 1945, in the center of his chest; I used to wish that the airplane distinguished me, age two, and my blue dress. But all that time growing up in Birmingham, when I studied the photograph, I shared a secret with my former self. Although it had escaped the colorist's brush, that seemingly pure hand of mine, resting with spread fingers, palm up on my knee, was sticky with chocolate ice cream. This is the earliest memory of food I have.

I remember we were hastily rounded up for the photograph (was it at a train station?) and I decided not to inconvenience others by asking them to wait while I washed my hand. Certainly, I didn't want anyone to regret the purchasing of my ice cream cone. Seated between my brothers, I turned my hand palm-up to try to keep the chocolate off my dress and knee. I decided not to look at my hand, to look out. Ever since, my hand, my conscience, and my chocolate have enjoyed an intimate relationship.

Is it any wonder that if you took my sacred childhood books from the shelf of my (now professional) library, you would find smears of chocolate pie in *David Copperfield* and *The Three Musketeers*? Those pies were homemade! The chocolate was cooked in a double boiler; the meringue on top was beaten with a flat wire whisk across a large, white platter with a gold-gilt border! Those implements were also used for making sunshine cake.

Ah, let us remember the preparation of meringue, essential to both chocolate pie and sunshine cake. The egg whites start clear and lank in the shallow declivity of the platter; when Mama tilts the platter they threaten to slide off, try to dribble like thin jelly over the rim. But no! Mama catches them in the curly wires, she whisks them back with brisk good humor, with confident power. She piles that runny matter back on itself; she feeds it air. At the very level of my eyes, it changes. From clear and repulsive it turns white and frothy, finally a heap of clouds, but with peaks and valleys—a mountainous terrain whose ranges are entirely snow-covered. Meringue.

In my novel, *Sherlock in Love*, Sherlock Holmes's violin teacher attempts to instruct Holmes on how to play a sixteen-note phrase in a waltz: "He informs Holmes that all sixteen have the shape of a little hill. 'A peak of meringue, if you please. It swoops up, and then it must swoop down. And the whole thing is full of air. What is meringue without the support of air?'" Could that teacher have been in the Jeter kitchen at some time, watching the creation of meringue?

Let us defer the sunshine cake, for sunshine cake keeps very well in memory while chocolate demands that we make frequent, obsessive returns to her domain. Upon a pond of chocolate waiting in a fluted pie crust, we mound that *overly* white mass of meringue—soon to be "browned" with a golden film, and, on the points and curlicues, the gold will become so deep as to be tipped with actual brown. The surface of the meringue will offer just the right texture, slightly resistant, to tongue and palate—best eaten warm while reading.

Now, if you ate such a piece of chocolate pie and read, simultaneously, Micawber's denunciation of Uriah HEEP, then, then the world was delicious, defined by justice—thwack goes Micawber's ruler!—resolute beauty, and complete—smack!—satisfaction.

Whenever I tried whipping whites into such a meringue, I found it too big a challenge. When the naughty whites did slip over the rim of the platter; my arm, not the whites, grew stiff. Shaking my head, I would turn the whisk back to Mama. "All that playing the violin," Mama explained sympathetically, "built up the muscle in my bow arm." But she no longer played the violin—too difficult to hold up through the pregnancies. Now we had the piano. When the neighborhood kids came over, at the request of Elizabeth Grady (who shared her parents' filched cigarettes with my brothers), Mama would leave off Chopin etudes, Bach fugues, and Beethoven sonatas to play the "Sabre Dance" so fast and loud, we were all satisfied, though we cried "Again!" and were again satisfied in our souls' need for adventure. Then she brought out the cookies—chocolate chip, or sugar cookies, or cocoa puffs, oatmeal and succulent raisin, or peanut butter with a crisscross from the fork tines on top and embodying the perfect texture between resistant crumb and soft butter.

Reading and eating, writers and food—how wise Linda Beattie was to let those pleasures resonate with one another in this book. What about the fiction that is in itself directly about the preparation or enjoyment of food? Have writers linked such food moments with that business which is of the utmost human importance, people creating among themselves a matrix of love and loyalty? I have tried to do so in my own fiction writing; for example, see "The Perfecting of the Chopin Valse No. 14 in E Minor" in my collection *Ice Skating at the North Pole* in which music, dinner-party food, and flowers transcend the threat of mortality. For an immortal rendering of a similar idea, see the dinner party at the climax of the first section of the great Virginia Woolf's *To the Lighthouse*, my favorite novel in the world. Dickens fortified the human spirit with hot punch; and "Was there ever such a goose?" as that in *A Christmas Carol*?

I am forever telling my fiction-writing students at the University of Louisville and at Vermont College, "Put in more food. Tell exactly what they ate. How was it prepared?" Surely the prize for such writing goes to a Kentucky novel-in-progress by my friend and former student, Cinda

Sullivan, who used to have a gourmet shop in Louisville, and whose literary dinners for a few of us lucky local writers cause writer/doctor Daly Walker, who knows the best restaurants of the east and west coasts, France, and Italy, to blush with pleasure in the eating. Though this page cannot present you with the food itself, it can convey the fragrance through Cinda's writing about Thanksgiving preparations in Kentucky: "Nonie blended country ham and onions and celery and sausage and the hickory nuts together in a heavy metal grinder that was clamped to the sinkboard. Mother dipped into a bubble-topped tin of oysters and lifted out a handful mounted on her palm, then layered the miniature, pearlized pillows on beds of saltine crumbs. Gabe soaked the turkey in the sink like a heavy, naked baby. All talk was of ingredients; the words were warm and smelled of sage.

"The arms and hands of her adults fascinated Clara. The way they moved. Nonie turned the grinder handle slowly, round and round at an even, steady speed. With her other palm, she caught the stuffing, one plump dollop at a time, and, molding as she moved, winding the handle as she molded, Nonie tucked the egg-shaped packets snugly into a glass baker which sat a few inches away. Mother's fingers lifted above and lightly in and out of her creamy oyster pudding as delicately as dancers on a cloud and Daddy's strong arms guided the slippery clean, fourteen-pound bird with such sure grace, it could have weighed an ounce."

I do think I could preach a sermon on the transcendence of such writing, of such cooking—and I think I know the church that would let me do it. First Unitarian of Louisville, whose early December Food Fair features minister Richard Beal's mother's recipe for a Maine plum pudding to which Dickens would gladly raise a holiday cup.

Oh, chocolate calls to me again, and I remember Royal pudding, which came in a small, compact box of such satisfying proportions that I think of that humble package along with the Parthenon. I am staring into the radio, lost, eating pudding, listening to the Lone Ranger, heralded by the trumpet fanfare of the *William Tell Overture.* Justice and warm chocolate ride again—please, let there be a lump, the prize of the pudding.

Oh, the Sweet of Childhood! And there were savory sweets outside the realm of chocolate. I haven't mentioned butter pies, made of scraps of from-scratch pie dough, placed on a cookie sheet, pricked with a fork, dotted with butter, sprinkled with a mixture of sugar and cinnamon. And I didn't mention the cherry pies—slightly tart—over-woven with butter-brushed latticework, some cherry probably harboring a pit. Nor did I mention morning pancakes, saturated with brown sugar dissolved into butter melted across the lacy brown tops. Nor did I mention cream of wheat.

With good reason, that last. Perhaps I was six. I was crouched in front of the fireplace, for warmth. (It got cold in Alabama—ask Wade Hall!) Our house in Birmingham was poorly insulated, chilly even with a well-stoked coal furnace. I loved the fireplace—so pioneer like—and before school, I crouched on the brick hearth, the plate of white cream of wheat before me, for breakfast. The pat of butter in the center became a house surrounded by snow. Yellow with lamplight, the house was being seen from above, I imagined, from a mountaintop with a view of the valley, and here came the snowplow, the spoon, to liberate the house. But to liberate a house: a rule. You must come first from the north, then in from each direction, east, south, quartering the snow, dawdling—till, suddenly—you were swooped up and spanked! (Utter amazement to be jerked from one world to another!)

To eat and image! To eat and read! Those should be the coordinates for bliss!

Cream of wheat clearly led to wickedness. Let us leave it and return to thoughts of chocolate.

Hot cocoa, with a capful of alcoholic vanilla! That was, at first, mainly for November 11, after Mama and I had come home cold on the city bus from watching the Armistice Day Parade, perhaps the largest one in the nation at that time. When I was in high school, after my father had died, my mother made me the hot cocoa to help me relax from my studies, "to go to sleep on," Mama would say. After drinking a cup of hot cocoa, my stomach became an inner pillow of warmth around which my whole being could curl. Now, I fix hot Quik, after a winter's day of teaching, with a capful of vodka.

That swooping up from the snowy cream of wheat?—that was my father, his patience at an end with my dawdling in the realms of imagination when first grade awaited.

The next morning after evenings when I had been disobedient enough to be scolded by my father, I might awake to find beside my head one of his thin socks distended with apples and oranges—a peace offering. Such had been the entirety of his Christmas as a boy, at times, and on our Christmas Eves my brothers and I always hung our ordinary socks, to be stuffed with tangerines and apples, pecans and English walnuts, from the holiday mantel—just below that watchful, fading, hand-tinted photograph of us. Each Christmas, of course, always took us further away from those children, the blue dress, the white airplane on a field of pinkish-buff. Daddy always provided, on Christmas, a box of Whitman's Sampler to be eaten while we opened the gifts.

Throughout the year, using Forever Yours chocolate bars, my father taught me, in a lesson so gentle that even now I am not sure he meant to teach me anything, to be responsible about my body. When he realized how much kids loved them, he would place in the fridge an open display boxful of them, about the size of a ream of typing paper. The candy was simply there in the open; the chocolate bars, neatly lined up in a double row in the box, were available, unpoliced, replaced when gone; the neighbor kids were in awe. Fresh and cold from the fridge, a Forever Yours still in the wrapper could be crackled across the edge of the counter: then you could see the strata of goodness—vanilla nougat, capped with a layer of caramel, the whole rectangle contained and outlined with dark chocolate, thicker on the top and standing, even in cross-section, in small dark peaks. I soon learned that happiness was eating one Forever Yours, discomfort came after two, and three resulted in running to the bathroom.

On most Sundays, like the Kentucky father in Cinda Sullivan's novel, Daddy cooked the Sunday chicken—perhaps given him by a patient in lieu of payment. On less frequent state occasions, if Uncle Dock and Aunt Jewell had come back to Alabama from Texas, we went across the driveway for dinner so that our elderly grandmother and an invalid aunt could get to the table. The food there was different—truly Deep South cooking, for my father, Aunt Pet, and Aunt Kumi (who taught high-school math and never married) and my grandmother Sena Sewanee Carter Jeter, after whom I am named, all had lived on a farm, some forty miles south of Montgomery, in Crenshaw County. The place was named Helicon, and they all wanted to go back there, and the family agreed that if they were scattered and war came, then they would all meet in the pine forest at Helicon, by the spring. The food: boiled okra, so slimy its main function was gagging children, chicken and boiled dumplings (too pale!), cornbread baked in a black iron skillet, biscuit (forever singular). But Aunt Kumi's hard, dry, flat savory teacake cookies were another matter. They were flavored with nutmeg—a flavor we did not use across the driveway, a flavor worth learning.

Aunt Pet's room—she was the invalid—was all flavor and aroma. On her bedside table, she kept packs of chewing gum—Spearmint in white,

Doublemint in the green wrapper, Juicy Fruit in yellow. I was to have any of it, all of it, whenever I wanted, as much as I could cram in my mouth. For aroma, Pet's array of cologne and perfume was at my disposal, just as generously as was the chewing gum. All of her necklaces could be worn at once, and all of the pins. The clip earrings I fastened over each fingernail. And while I sat chewing away, more vigorously than a young cow with her favorite cud, Aunt Pet would tell me stories of mad dogs loose in South Alabama and of haints who lived in the attic at her Grandpa's and whose function it was to guard the gold in the hollow log trough over the door. What did they eat? I asked. "Haints don't have to eat. Oh, if you reached up toward the lintel, then Slim Jim, with his long bony hands and long claws, would reach down from the loft to rake at you." Slim Jim being a haint and me being a developing skeptic, I demanded she draw a picture of him. She did, her arthritic hands unable to close over the pencil, but holding the fingers out straight, her hands trembling, she drew. How she could draw! My brother John got that talent, which he has always exercised with the tip of his tongue touching the corner of his mouth—as though tasting something nice. Bejeweled, stinking to high heaven, I sat entranced, absorbing tales of the old South. I felt I didn't live in the true South at all; that was farther south, Helicon. Sometimes, Pet would pause in her storytelling to swallow, for strength, a raw egg in a glass of orange juice, brought to her by the maid.

A double garage hulked at the head of the driveway shared by our bungalow and the relatives' mirror-image bungalow. After dark, knowing I feared the black garage interior with its wide-spread doors and the bad man who might crouch there beside the cars, Aunt Kumi would always say, "Run fast, Sena. I'll watch you till you get in." Clutching the white cloth napkin-wrapped teacake cookies Kumi would be sending over to my father, often too tired to come over to chat, I ran like the wind, saying to myself "like the wind, like the wind" till I leapt to the concrete pad before the three wooden steps to the back door.

At home, my mother might be sitting in the living room peeling apples—winesap or red delicious—with a knife, which she called "my good little paring knife," into a perforated tin strainer. My brothers would be sitting across the room, waiting. When she finished a piece of apple, she threw it hard as a baseball to one of them. With a juicy smack, the apple would thunk the palm of a hand held like a fielder's mitt. Sometimes she would throw wild, and Marvin or John would have to dive for it. They never missed, even if they snagged the apple just above an arabesque in the worn rug. Over there, across the driveway, was gentility. At home, we threw apples if it would help you practice your fielding.

At home, I had been allowed to draw on the walls, if so moved. At home, if we had an elaborate array of cars spread out on the living room floor, or my tin cowboy town and neighboring ranch needed space, they might remain there for days, my mother ignoring the vacuum, stepping carefully over our toys to get to the piano.

At home, I was allowed to eat my food with my fingers. My school lunches contained hand-held items, transported in a paper sack with *Sena* writ large on both sides in Mama's confident script. When I went to high school, I decided it was time to wield knife and fork, but I was so clumsy that I could only choose foods from the cafeteria line that were easy to fork—green beans, mainly. I could scarcely cut meat. Mama cut my pork chops into bites of beautiful size for me, with her good little paring knife—perhaps too sharp for precious-me to wield. (When we were small, my father bought only furniture with rounded corners and edges, lest we dash out an eye against one.)

Once, about age ten, as usual I held the pork-chop plate vertical before my face, all ready to lick the pleasant grease, when an odd thought occurred: "Is it all right for me to do this?" I asked. Mama answered. "Lick it if you want to. It's good for you." (I was a very skinny kid.) Then she added as an afterthought, "You might not want to do it in public." We were barely conventional in other matters—no set bedtimes, baths mentioned gently only once a week, no problems if clothes came home dirty from play, dinner (except for Sunday) kept warm on the stove to be eaten at any eater's convenience. A favorite supper food was fish cakes, and I shall provide that recipe. School (I don't think I was ever tardy), homework, and play were important; maintenance functions could be fitted around them.

But with all my rhapsodizing over the ghosts of times and foods past and present, I find that I have neglected to tell you much about sunshine cake, which is the recipe I most associate with my mother, for I have never eaten it except when she cooked it or as I cooked it, once, for brother Marvin's fiftieth birthday. It is the special, author's recipe that will follow.

But first I must describe the cake to you. It is a sponge cake, quite tall and yellow, baked in a tube pan. My mother never frosted it, but the crust on the top of the cake is a golden brown, and it is the most delicious part of the cake. In the crust, one has essence of cake, I think, a sort of concentration of flavor and unique texture. The tall interior of the cake has a bubbly texture; it holds a lot of air. Though we usually think of air as conveying sunshine, here sunshine has become myriad yellow pockets containing air. I have always thought of sunshine cake as a big cake, both because of its height—a real bank of sunshine there—and because it was the only dessert my mother mixed in her biggest opaque glass bowl—the yellow one. (Chocolate chip cookies came from the green, medium-sized one.) Do you remember the large, white platter and the flat, wire whisk with which she beat meringue for chocolate pie? They reappear in this scene, for with sunshine cake, you separate the eggs, beat the whites till they stand in peaks (on the platter), and then fold them gently into the rest of the mixture in the yellow bowl. Fold together like a fiction writer folds together memory and imagination. You had better have a good arm for the whites—did you play the violin?—or, I suppose, an electric mixer, though such an item offends memory as an anachronism.

But why, suddenly, does sunshine cake make me think of starlight? Perhaps I do not wish to conclude my mixing here, not quite ready to put this confection in the oven of *Savory Memories*.

Imagine a summer night, and we—the two boys and the girl, the parents, perhaps Uncle Dock—are camped at the head of the red-clay driveway before the double garage; my father is superintending the creation of homemade ice cream. Aunt Kumi drags out one of her mahogany chairs to sit with the group around the freezer. On the side of the wooden bucket is a small hole where salty water slushes out; my brothers are valiantly cranking away. When I try to turn the handle, Daddy puts his hand over mine to help. After our turn at the freezer, my father asks me if I can see Orion, and we study the night sky. He points out the Dipper. Though light spills into the driveway from our back door and from the kitchen of my aunts (they are both still alive though my grandmother has died by the time I have this memory), I believe that we are mostly turning the crank by starlight. As the liquid inside the gleaming inner-bucket freezes toward solid, the crank gets harder and harder to turn. Aunt Kumi tells of a star out there, beyond our seeing, of such multiples of size that it is frightening to imagine it. I move closer in the circle, place my finger in the drain hole which I associate with a navel. The water is colder than cold. I lick my salty finger. I know that soon the freezer will be dismantled and the lid will be carefully removed from the inner container so as not to let salt in; I know that the dasher with its many little paddles will be pulled out and handed me to lick. The ice cream is always vanilla, always so cold it makes me dizzy. The starry coldness of outer space has gotten in it.

If one is about to eat Mama's sunshine cake, whose mind wouldn't leap to Daddy's starlit ice cream?

The cake is eaten warm as sunshine, though the recipe advises inverting the pan for cooling. We only allowed so much cooling—till we could handle the pan. A cake slice holds together nicely if you pick it up in your hand—no need for the civilizing fork—and bite into its wedge.

Only once do I remember disaster with the cake. My mother's beloved Aunt Lucy and Aunt Lizzie, my great-aunts, authentically old with white hair and crooked backs, were coming down from the North, for a stopover during their train trip to Florida, where they would winter in St. Petersburg and watch the Yankees' spring training, take snapshots of Babe Ruth. How excited my mother was! Some of her people. And it was her fiftieth birthday—I was still a little girl, my parents having married late and having had children very late. (Perhaps that is why they were so permissive with us.) Alas, when she baked sunshine cake for the aunts, she forgot to switch the oven from preheat to bake, and that marvelous top crust was burnt black as a cinder.

"Boy Howdy!" my mother exclaimed. Then, rallying, "Well, I'll just slice off the top. The rest's cooked perfectly well." And she did. Her family was with her. That was the main thing. My mother beaming, we all ate our cake with pleasure, as I hope you do, around the table, mouthful after mouthful of moist sunshine.

Flora Lee Sims Jeter's Sunshine Cake

one nine- or ten-inch ungreased tube pan, in two parts
one cup, sifted before measuring, cake flour
six to seven eggs
one and one-fourth cups sugar
one teaspoon vanilla
one-half teaspoon cream of tartar

Preheat the oven to 350 degrees. Separate the eggs. In a large bowl, beat the egg yolks; add vanilla and sifted flour. On a large, flat, white platter, using a flat whisk, whip the egg whites, adding the cream of tartar and the sugar, till the whites are stiff and stand in peaks. Gently fold the egg whites into the flour mixture, a little at a time. The whole thing is full of air. What is sunshine cake without the support of air? Pour the mixture into the tube pan. Change electric stove from preheat to bake and bake for forty-five to fifty minutes. Invert the pan to cool till pan can be safely handled. Run a knife around to loosen the side and tube adhesions; push the cake out. Place on cake plate for a bit more cooling. If two children are nearby, hand one the tube and the other the sides of the baking pan. The crumbs are delicious. Cut the cake with a cake knife with large serrations—serrations like the scallops you would make if you were drawing a stylized sea.

Mama Jeter's Fish Cakes

one nine-ounce can of chunk light tuna in spring water
sixteen saltine crackers
two eggs
one-half onion, chopped (optional)
two stalks celery, cut up (optional)
enough cooking oil to cover the bottom of a heavy skillet, about one-eighth
    to one-fourth inch

From the tuna, drain the water and discard. In a medium mixing bowl, green perhaps in color, crush the crackers. Add the tuna and the eggs. Stir together. Add the onion and celery, if you like those flavors. Form patties, not too large or they'll break apart. You can cover them and store in the refrigerator till nearer suppertime, if you like. Heat the oil in the skillet till the temperature will sizzle a tiny drop of water. Carefully place the fish cakes into the oil. Turn once. Remove from the cooking oil as soon as the fish cakes are golden and place on a plate with a paper towel to absorb extra oil. If you like, you can concoct a sauce mixing Miracle Whip, ranch dressing, and dill weed. Some people like ketchup. Fish cakes can be kept warm easily and well in the top half of a double boiler, if the members of your family eat serially, when the spirit urges.

～Sena Jeter Naslund has published two short story collections (*Ice Skating at the North Pole* and *The Disobedience of Water*) and two novels (*The Animal Way to Love* and *Sherlock in Love*). A resident of Louisville, she has received grants from the National Endowment for the Arts, the Kentucky Arts Council, and the Kentucky Foundation for Women. At the University of Louisville, she holds the title of University Distinguished Teaching Professor, and she is also on the faculty of the MFA in Writing Program of Vermont College. For twenty years, she has edited *The Louisville Review*.

When Angels Comb Their Hair

LEE PENNINGTON

The blizzard of 1996 which was lovely white in the trees and covered scars of the neighborhood where I now live was a reminder of something past, something of childhood, and the coming down sent my mind dancing across the years to Greenup County, Kentucky, where I grew up, to the head of that narrow valley and the mostly log house sitting flush against the hillside.

The window at the back let in very little light—the window opening out directly onto the hill—and in the late autumn we had to remove the leaves piled up against the glass, and likewise remove the snow that sometimes covered everything, to let in any light at all. Until 1947 when electricity came, once the kerosene lamp was blown out, darkness was personified.

Until I was eight, I lived in the "big" house, along with the rest of the family. That was the year my mother had a "discussion" with me, she becoming leery of the pet snakes (two copperheads, one rattlesnake, and one blacksnake) and the black widow spiders I kept in gallon jars under my bed. Mom and Dad granted all their eleven children an exceptional amount of independence and freedom to pursue various adventures and activities so long as the freedom and independence didn't infringe on others.

The pets, Mom felt, fell into the last category.

She didn't say I couldn't have them. She simply said, "I don't mind your keeping your rock collection in the house. But the snakes and spiders, I'm afraid they might get loose. So if you want to stay with your pets, you'll have to move out of the house."

I opted to go to the meat shed which had a nice shelf, and I cut away a third of a mattress, placed the other two-thirds on the shelf and had a nice, if fairly high, bed. The pets had plenty of room in their jars on the floor under the bed-shelf.

The thing I missed most from then on was the against-the-hill window where I often watched snow pile bright white until the light was gone. The meat shed had no window.

However, in the new setting I imagined listening to the sound of falling snow. Perhaps I really could hear it fall; I'm not sure. At least I thought I could, just as I believed on a quiet summer night, under a sky bundle of stars, I could hear corn grow.

Snow back then was always a glorious event. And I'm inclined to think, listening to local weather forecasters and hearing the glee in their voices as they predict a snowfall, it still is. Also, I'm sure there must be some atavistic collective consciousness we all have concerning our special relationship with snow. The sleigh rides, the making of angels, the jumping into giant piles wherever we find them, of creating human figures and making up songs about them—all these things attest to something greater than weather too cold for rain.

In the urban hustle, snow is a travel deterrent—something to tell us to slow down with bent fenders presented here and there as punctuation.

The snow of my past was no such thing.

Snow was freedom. Even deep snow.

I remember one fall of more than two feet, and my father and I took short boards and wrapped burlap bags around them, bound our feet to them, and made snowshoes of sorts and set out to a neighbor's house a mile away. I remember thinking, "When it snows, you no longer have to stay in the road."

When it snowed, I also caught birds.

I'm not sure why I caught birds; I always turned them loose. Yet, I remember many a snow where I swept away a spot in the white, put crumbled-up cornbread on the spot, propped up one end of a wooden box with a small stick and put the box over the cornbread, tied a long string to the stick and extended the string back to a slightly raised window where I sat inside the house and watched until enough birds got to eating and I jerked the string—dropping the box. Sometimes I caught five or six birds at one pull. Then, I went outside, turned them loose, and re-set the box trap.

I also tracked rabbits in the snow and learned early the triangle-like two holes at one point and one hole at another meant the rabbit was traveling in the direction of the two footprints. If I followed the tracks long enough, I found the rabbit sitting. Although it's been many years since I hunted (the last time was when I was sixteen), I still enjoy following the two tracks, one track until I find the sitting ball of fur and am spiritually rejuvenated.

When snow reached the melting stage, it sometimes told me a direction if I were lost. The north side of the hill held the snows longer. I could always tell the north side and by deduction the south side.

Rabbits appeared to know about the north side, south side also. When tracking them on the remaining melting snow of the north side, the tracks always--that's always--led to the south side and then ended where there was no more snow. I never once saw tracks come into snow on the north side; they always were leaving.

But the thing I remember most about snow—more than catching birds, more than tracking rabbits, more than wading in the winter wonder—happened every time there was a fall deep enough to scrape up spoonfuls.

It was snow cream. Mom made snow cream.

The first flake down, spotted by the children snow-watchers who made the announcement, started an anticipation that was most always filled with a prayer or two to "get it deep enough, oh, please make it deep enough." That anticipation reached crescendo when Mom sent one of us outside with a big dipping spoon and two milk buckets to get things started. Often we had to return for refills once the making process got well under way and the snow from the buckets disappeared into the mixing bowl.

We watched Mom stir and mix, mix and stir, taste a spoonful, stir, and mix some more. Then it was our turn.

The first taste was incredible! It is one of those delectable experiences you just don't forget—like the feeling you have when a snowflake lights and melts on your nose.

During the 1996 blizzard as I watched snow blanket and then add quilts to my yard, the almost-forgotten urge from my youth returned.

I wanted snow cream.

I had, I thought, everything I needed to make the stuff and once again shake hands with my childhood. The snow was certainly deep enough. I had a big dipper and buckets, even if they weren't milk buckets.

I am also past the stage where I worry much anymore about things like strontium ninety, captured in the white down fall, getting me. If I wanted snow cream, I was, by gosh, going to have it and hang the pollution and my impending death. I was going to make snow cream!

Only one ingredient was missing. I had forgotten how to make snow cream. I knew you needed snow and sugar and vanilla flavoring and maybe milk, but I didn't remember how much and in what order the things went together.

So right in the middle of the blizzard (well, at least eight inches of snow were already down) I called home to ask Boots, my sister, and Mom, now ninety-six years old, how to make snow cream. Boots had learned how from Mom, and Mom had learned from Grandmother and so on back to Eve, probably.

"Yes," said Mom. "I still remember how to make it. You go get you a big bucket of snow."

"Every time it snows," said Boots, "the kids" (they're all adults now, with families of their own, but she still calls them kids) "want me to make snow cream. I used to worry about the snow being polluted, but decided something's gonna get us all, eventually, anyway, so why worry about it?"

After they told me how to make snow cream, I discovered I was missing another ingredient—canned milk or evaporated milk.

It was nearly a mile to the nearest quick-and-open-all-the-time store, the car was imprisoned in the garage, and I felt like a certain beer commercial concerning a man heading over several snow-covered miles just to get a cold one. I bundled up, snow-boots and all, and headed out, trudging through white wonder over the back lots and down across Shelbyville Road.

I found the can of cream and the lady looked surprised that I hadn't come for anything else, so I said to her, "You can't make snow cream without cream."

"My God," she said. "Are you going to make snow cream?"

"I am."

"I haven't had snow cream since I was a kid," she said as her eyes and mind wandered somewhere.

I invited her back with me to share snow cream, and for a moment she looked like she was going to take me up on the offer, but she didn't.

"I'm not going to eat any," my wife Joy said to me when I got the gourmet dish from the sky finished.

"Why not?"

"Eggs. The raw eggs."

I didn't think too long of the hazards of salmonella. The stuff just looked too good. And besides, the gallon I had just made was barely enough to whet my appetite and set me waiting again for the angels to comb their hair.

Snow Cream

(Enough to make one mixing bowl full and feed five or six kids or one man remembering childhood)

three raw eggs
one large can of evaporated milk
two teaspoons vanilla flavoring
one and one-half cups sugar
dash of salt
big bucket of snow

Beat eggs until they are "fluffy." Add can of evaporated milk or pint of cream and mix well. Add flavoring. Add dash of salt. Add sugar; mix. Begin adding snow and keep adding and mixing until the snow cream reaches the consistency you like. Any snow cream left over (not likely there'll be any) can be frozen. When taken out of freezer, the snow cream needs to be re-beaten to get the consistency back. You can also experiment, according to my sister, with putting fruit in the mixture.

From my recent experience, I also suggest gathering the snow in a place not too close to hemlock trees and falling needles.

∾Lee Pennington has tried his hand at many things—poetry, drama, fiction, folksinging, storytelling, teaching, videomaking, and even cooking, although he admits very close to total failure at cooking. He is the author of nineteen books including *Scenes from a Southern Road*, *Songs of Bloody Harlan*, *The Scotian Women*, *Appalachia My Sorrow*, *Coalmine*, and the *Janus Collection*. His poetry collections *I Knew a Woman* (1977) and his most recent *Thigmotropism* (1993) were both nominated for the Pulitzer Prize. In 1984 the state legislature named him a Poet Laureate of Kentucky. He and his wife Joy are both professors of English at Jefferson Community College in Louisville, Kentucky.

Mama's Favorite

Betty Layman Receveur

I was brought up by my paternal grandparents. My grandmother, who had a gentle voice and the most beautiful smile I ever saw, was five feet four inches tall, and nicely rounded in face and body. My grandfather was six feet five, long and lean, with highcheek bones and a Roman nose that bespoke the Cherokee blood of his great-grandmother. I'm sure there were those who thought them a mismatched pair, what with the difference in body build and height, but I didn't. I knew that they loved each other dearly, and I knew that they loved me.

We lived in Louisville, on Sixth Street, two doors from St. Louis Bertrand Catholic grade school—where I attended classes during the school year. The church was on the other side of the school, the rectory beyond the church on the corner of Sixth and St. Catherine. On hot summer evenings, we would sit on our front porch to catch the breeze—no air conditioning then—and the neighbors would stroll by, stopping to lean on the tops of the black, iron-railed fence and talk awhile. Sometimes the Dominican priests from the rectory would come sit on the porch with us, and my grandmother would bring out cool glasses of tea—or lemonade on those rare occasions when we had a lemon or two.

Though we had little in the way of money, I never felt poor. My grandmother—*Mama*—and I always did things together. She was creative at coming up with ways to do things cheaply. For instance, when the linoleum on our kitchen floor wore right through to the brown backing, we went to the hardware store and bought two cans of paint—one blue, one green. First we applied the green paint. Once it was dry, we took a much-used sponge, dipped it in the blue paint, and made lovely patterns on the green. We had to redo it every year or so, but that just meant we could change colors.

Together, we did the laundry in our old wringer washer, then rinsed the clothes in a laundry tub. Some of the pieces, such as Granddaddy's shirts, or pillow cases, we starched—you had to cook starch back then; no aerosol cans. The wash was then hung to dry on the line in our backyard. The next day, we sprinkled down the pieces we'd starched the day before, and rolled them in a towel to dampen evenly before we began the ironing, which took several hours. We cleaned our house, we did dishes together, we did errands together—and we *cooked.*

I remember food and its daily preparation as a meaningful part of our lives. There were no frozen dinners, no quick-fix meals to be picked up at the supermarket. If there were any supermarkets then, I didn't know about them. If my memory serves me correctly, there was a store a couple of blocks from where we lived, but it only had one counter and an old cash register whose tinny keys needed to be punched twice sometimes before the amount popped up. The proprietor and his wife knew virtually every customer who came in.

Though our food budget was modest, Mama could make the least expensive foods taste wonderful. We had beans often. She preferred great northerns or pintos, and together we would pick through them in the evening, making sure that any small stones were thrown away. The rinsed beans were soaked in a big pot overnight, then put on the stove to simmer half the day, with a piece of jowl bacon and a whole onion added along with the other seasonings.

I would help stir up the cornbread batter for supper—as we called it then. Mama would caution me to stand back as she emptied it into the old iron skillet, where an inch or more of hot bacon fat bubbled and smoked and spat as the batter invaded it. The skillet would then go into a hot oven, and the finished bread came out with an incredibly delicious, thick, dark crust, the inside tender and crumbly. Slaw, made with shredded cabbage and a carrot or two, topped with vinegar-and-sugar dressing, would round out our meal. It is only now that I realize how nutritious it was, as well as satisfying.

To some, it might seem that we did nothing but work, but that wasn't the case. Sometimes we'd walk downtown together and stroll along Fourth Street, stopping in the five-and-dime stores—Newberry's, McCrory's, Woolworth's—buying a spool of thread or a bar of soap that smelled especially nice—the soap was usually for me. Sometimes we just looked. If we had money enough, we would go to the food counter at McCrory's or Newberry's and have a hot dog with mustard and relish, and a root beer for lunch. Sometimes, we would walk to the White Castle for hamburgers.

My grandfather was a man who worked long and hard for the wages he brought home. I'm sure he was tired at the end of the day, but he always made time for me. On his day off, he never failed to walk with me to the Cabbage Patch settlement several blocks out Sixth Street. There was a branch library there, which opened two days a week. They limited the number of books a child could take to five. I always had my five read long before time to return them.

On our way back from those ventures, Granddaddy and I would stop at the drugstore on the corner nearest to our house. At the soda fountain, I would sit on one of the high stools, marveling at the cool, slick feel of the white marble counter. The straws stood tall in their heavy glass container, its chrome lid shiny as a mirror. The white paper napkins were equally correct in their dispenser box. I remember the faint smell of chocolate syrup and maraschino cherries that always seemed to linger in the air. Granddaddy would buy me a cherry coke, then wait patiently as I slowly sipped that wondrous treat, making it last as long as possible.

In the summer, we would go down on Jefferson Street to the haymarket. A neighbor had an automobile, and we would all go together, to stroll along the tables of fresh vegetables and fruits, of eggs and milk, and whatever else the farmers brought to town. Sometimes there were fresh flowers, or even litters of puppies to be given away. We would take home potatoes—sweet and Irish—green beans and onions and assorted other vegetables. Mama always watched for the first apples of the year—June apples, she called them. She said they made the best fried pies. Granddaddy said hers were the best he'd ever tasted anyway, June apples or no.

One summer, when we had saved some money and Granddaddy had some time off, the three of us took the bus down to Marion County, where two of Mama's sisters lived on farms—not far from one another. Aunt Lee Buckman and her husband, Ollie, had fourteen children, the youngest of which, a girl, was four or five years older than I. Aunt Cora Luckett and her husband, Tom, had a son and three daughters. The youngest daughter, Theresa, and I were nearest in age. Only two years older, she was always a favorite of mine, and we are still close to this day.

Our visit that day coincided with the ripening of wild blackberries. The men hitched up the horses to flatbed wagons, and all of us, aunts and uncles and cousins, rode out to where the dark fruit hung heavy. We returned, sunburned and chigger-bitten, but with washtubs full to the brim.

Most of the berries would be made into jams and jellies, but that night there were cobblers the size of dishpans, enough to feed us all, juices oozing from slits in the crusts to form deep, gelatinous purple patterns against the flaky pastry.

I remember watching one morning as Aunt Lee made a batch of her famous buttermilk biscuits. She mixed them in a huge dough bowl, the likes of which would bring a pretty penny on the antique market now. It has been a long time since I tasted such biscuits.

Aunt Cora was equally great at breakfasts. She'd fry country ham in her iron skillet, then after piling slices high on an ironstone platter, she'd make red-eye gravy to ladle over the succulent ham when it reached the individual plates. I can still smell that ham, still feel the chewy texture of it in my mouth. I have been a vegetarian for several years, now, but I must admit that I still miss country ham.

As I grew older, times became better. Wages were higher, and the lives of my grandparents were easier. After I married and started my family, I began to invite my grandparents to come to my home for the holiday meals. Mama loved to bake, and she always brought a cake. Usually Mrs. Creason's jam cake.

Her favorite cook in the world was the great Cissy Gregg, who was food editor at the *Courier-Journal* from 1942 to 1963. On two different occasions in the 1950s, the paper issued collections of Cissy's recipes. I still have copies of both of them. Tattered though they may be, I treasure them. Among all the great recipes in those pages—Mrs. Creason's Jam Cake among them—I found my own special cake. It wasn't attributed to anyone in particular. It was simply called Pound Cake, but it has proven to be the favorite of my sons and grandsons. We cannot have a holiday or a special occasion without it, but I often bake Mama's favorite, as well, and there is seldom a crumb left.

Both of my grandparents died in the early 1960s. Granddaddy first, then Mama two years later. I miss them terribly, still. I would not be a writer today if it weren't for them; my years with them were rich in everything that mattered.

Mrs. Creason's Jam Cake

This luscious, rich cake was attributed to Mrs. Herman Creason of Benton, Kentucky. My grandmother always made caramel frosting, and she used blackberry jam. I've made this cake with strawberry jam and found it to be delicious, as well. Also, I just grease the pans and dust lightly with flour instead of using paper liners.

five eggs, beaten
two cups sugar
three cups flour
one cup butter or shortening
one cup buttermilk
one teaspoon soda
one-fourth teaspoon salt
one-half teaspoon cinnamon
one and one-half teaspoons allspice
one cup raisins or chopped dates
one cup chopped nuts
one cup jam

Cream butter and gradually add the sugar until mixture is light and fluffy. Add well-beaten eggs. Sift flour before measuring and add to it the spices and the salt. Dissolve soda in buttermilk and add it and the flour mixture alternately to the egg-sugar-butter mixture and beat after each addition. Lightly dredge the fruit and nuts with extra flour and add them, with the jam, to the butter mixture. Stir to get good distribution.

Grease and paper-line two nine-inch cake pans—our batter filled the pans to their brims. Bake at 325 degrees for forty minutes. Cool layers on racks. Ice with caramel icing or whatever you like.

This same cake recipe was reprinted in the 1985 edition of *The Courier-Journal Kentucky Cookbook*. The following recipe for caramel frosting attributed in 1978 to Deni Hamilton was included.

Caramel Frosting

one and one-half cups firmly packed light brown sugar
pinch of salt
one cup butter
three-fourths cup flour
one cup heavy cream
one teaspoon vanilla

Mix sugar and flour. Cream butter until light and add sugar mixture, beating well. Mix in heavy cream and put in top of double boiler over boiling water. Stir constantly, and cook until about the thickness of medium cream sauce. Takes about fifteen minutes after it melts. Allow to cool completely after cooking. Sets up after it's on the cake for a couple of hours.

Pound Cake

This is the most beautiful cake I've ever made. The batter is even beautiful. Everyone who tastes it loves it. The recipe below is not the original cake recipe that appeared in Cissy Gregg's book. I have changed it over the years so that it contains less saturated fat, and I've never had a single complaint from my family. Instead of butter, I use Parkay margarine—the sixteen-ounce, four-stick package, which is marked 70 percent vegetable oil spread. Instead of cream, I use skim milk. The only other change I've made is to add the almond extract—along with the original vanilla. You'll love it!

one pound Parkay margarine
two and two-thirds cups sugar (a little more than a pound)
three and one-half cups flour (a little less than a pound)
eight eggs
eight tablespoons skim milk
one teaspoon pure vanilla extract
one teaspoon pure almond extract

Separate eggs. Whip egg whites until they begin to stiffen, then add six tablespoons of the sugar slowly (I do one tablespoon at a time, or the whites will fall), beating as you add. Continue beating until the mixture forms stiff peaks. Place in the refrigerator until the rest of cake is mixed.

Cream the margarine, add the remaining sugar, and beat until light. Add egg yolks two at a time, beating well after each addition. Add small amounts of flour and milk alternately, beating well. Add extracts, beat again. Fold in whites by hand, with an over-and-under motion, turning the mixing bowl as you go until the whites are incorporated, but the batter is still light. Don't over fold. Pour batter into a large, greased and floured, ten-inch tube pan. I spray my pan liberally with canola oil, then dust with flour just as liberally, turning the pan and dusting until all inner surfaces are covered. Shake out any excess flour.

Bake at 300 degrees for one hour and twenty-five minutes. Take from oven and place on a rack to cool. Don't be surprised when your cake falls an inch or so the first few minutes after it comes out of the oven. It's supposed to. That's what gives it that great texture. After cooling for forty-five minutes to an hour, turn the pan upside down, catching the cake on your hand—it should come out easily. Turn it right side up and continue to cool on rack until cake is completely cooled. Wrap in foil to keep fresh.

❧Betty Layman Receveur is a native Louisvillian best known for her historical novels, *Oh, Kentucky!* and *Kentucky Home*. In addition to having published five books, Receveur serves on the advisory board of Green River Writers, Inc., and teaches in creative writing workshops throughout Kentucky. The productions of which she claims to be most proud are her three sons, her four grandsons, her step-grandson, and her step-granddaughter.

One Writer's Beginning

FREDERICK SMOCK

My grandmother's house in Old Louisville, where I lived as a child, had a small backyard that sloped abruptly to a brick alley. Her garage was dug into the hillock, its flat roof only a step up from the yard, and the front lip of that roof made a wonderful vantage point—a dreamy spot to lie on my stomach and look out over the maze of little streets and houses teeming with children and cats and delivery trucks and laundry snapping in the magnolia-scented breeze.

The house across the alley held many mysteries. Never an adult came or went, and an army of children played or squabbled in the dirt yard among a scruffy menagerie of dogs and chickens. I would lie on my garage roof, my chin on my arms, and imagine their inner lives, inside that clapboard house, inside their tousled heads. It was this enchanted watching, I suppose, that began my education as a writer.

Sometimes today, on my way downtown, I detour through that alley. The house and garage are still there, and I glance up as I drive past to see if perhaps there is some new boy up on that roof, watching me.

I count it a lucky accident to have grown up in my grandmother's house. My own mother became the doyenne of the household, a gravitational star among the great-aunts and female cousins. And, for a time, I existed as the only child in this small community of protective women. It was a sort of pediatric harem.

The men in our family were all dead or gone. Gone to find their fortune, or their reward. I did not notice their absence until much later on. "Men come and go," an aunt remarked once, "women are the place." She made that remark in the kitchen, and I remember how it hung in the air, like a sharp aroma. Even now I can call it to mind: cinnamon, burnt.

My grandmother and her sister, whom she affectionately called "Sister," were well mated for widowhood. One pieced, the other quilted. One washed, the other dried. One did windows, the other floors. It was a house of working women, make no mistake—washing, darning, ironing, sweeping, waxing, airing, cooking . . .

Mattie and Iley were farm women, only recently moved from Owen County to the city. They lived out-of-doors as much as possible. They kept chickens in the backyard, and Iley, big as she was, could move like the wind and chase down a chicken and break its neck with a snap of her fingers, and she had a special recipe for frying it up:

fresh chicken (preferably killed and cleaned that day)
one big bowl of buttermilk
one big bowl of Gold Medal flour
Crisco oil
towels for draining

The secret to her recipe is the buttermilk, into which the chicken parts are dipped before dredging in flour, and frying in a cast-iron skillet over medium heat.

Saying "recipe" is misleading, perhaps, because it implies an orderly plan, and Iley's style of cookery was creative and chaotic. Or perhaps she was simply messy. She proceeded with dashes of this and handfuls of that, moving amid clouds of flour dust, bubbling grease, whistling steam. There was always a great clanging of pots and pans, and she sang along, or loudly hummed. Long strands of her frizzy gray hair strayed from her hairnet. In the building heat, her pale face flushed, and an aura, or halo, seemed to form about the soft contours of her ample body, signifying a source of unearthly energy just when she might have needed it most.

To my young mind, she seemed more a conjurer than a cook. For out of the whirlwind of the kitchen would come a splendid array of dishes: Bowls of green beans (with ham and onions). Bowls of mashed potatoes (churned with butter, sweet milk, and pepper). A small tureen of thick brown gravy. A bowl of kale, or mixed greens, still smelling of the earth, and spiced with vinegar and garlic, and sometimes cooked tomatoes. Baskets of toasty, cigar-shaped cornbread. Platters of fried chicken and corn-on-the-cob and, on special occasions, fresh tomatoes with crumbled bleu cheese.

At every Sunday dinner, in the middle of the table, in a bowl of water, floated a single magnolia blossom, cut from the tree in our front yard. Its perfume, layered between the chicken and the kale, is still what Sundays smell like. I have only to pass a magnolia tree in bloom and am transported back to #11 Innis Court, with its wide front porch, and the glider looking across the street to the broad flat lawn of the old folks' home, the Altenheim, and long afternoons idled away in delectable anticipation of the dinner hour.

It is curious to me now that we never ate out-of-doors, alfresco, as the Italians say, much as we worked and played in the open air. But these kinfolk of mine came from northern stock, from the crags and cairns of Scotland, long ago, where warmth and comfort are precious commodities.

The dinner hour, to boot, was always a civilized affair. It was meant to be conducted properly, and any meal conducted properly needed upright chairs, cloth napkins, overhead light, and perhaps most important, the ordering principle of a long oval table.

My job, as a boy, was to roam the length and breadth of our little cul-de-sac, to wear myself out with wonder.

No other children lived on our street. Only war widows, nuns, and a few old men. So I found my fellow creatures in the sprites that lived in the limestone walls, and in the spirits of the elephant trees on the broad Altenheim lawn, and in the animus of the clouds in our little patch of sky. Although my world lay bound to that one short street, my legs found no end of places to go.

We were poor, I imagine, but poverty is the natural condition of childhood. What want has a child of money? I was penniless and radiant, borne along by the heart's peasant song.

At night, cross-eyed weary, I dropped into my narrow bunk and was lulled to sleep by the lowing of the far Butchertown trains; the soft revolution of carlight on the ceiling; those magnolia-scented breezes. The dinner's aromas lingered in the darkened house, and also the faintest echoes of the clanging of pots and pans, and Iley's humming voice.

It was my job to dream deep and well-nourished dreams, to float along the rivers of Babylon, where all of life's wonders fill the night sky with bright and terrifying colors, and where a boy's hopes and fears are daubed on the blue dome of the mind.

All this was good and necessary training. For it seems to me that I write not to attempt to explain the world, but rather to deepen its mystery, to unfold, like a blown rose, its power to enchant. Science will explain the world to us. But art, like religion, like cookery, like childbirth, teaches us how inexplicable the world is.

∽Frederick Smock is a Kentucky native and a graduate of Georgetown College and the University of Louisville. He is the author of two books of poems, *12 Poems* and *Gardencourt* (both published by Larkspur Press), and a travel memoir, *This Meadow of Time: A Provence Journal* (Sulgrave Press). His poems and essays have been published in *Poetry*, the *Iowa Review*, *International Quarterly*, *American Literary Review*, and *Beaux Arts*, among others. In 1984, he and Sallie Bingham founded *The American Voice*, a pan-American literary journal that is published in Louisville, Kentucky. In 1995, he was awarded an Al Smith Fellowship in Poetry from the Kentucky Arts Council. He lives in Louisville with his wife Jackie and their two sons, Sam and Ben.

Good Eats with
Jane Martin and
Her Trustee

Alexander Speer

Actors Theatre of Louisville has been the site of the premieres of many plays written by Kentucky's nationally acclaimed playwright, the mysterious and fiercely reclusive Jane Martin. Now she has been asked to write down some of her food memories for this book. As her legal representative and public spokesman, I suppose I know as much about her as anyone. Well, actually I know *more* about her than anyone, except Jane herself, of course. Although Jane is a very private person and doesn't like to talk about herself, I'm going to reveal a few facts about her. First, I can tell you that Jane does, indeed, live in Kentucky, and that her inspiration and subjects generally come from this area, as you will know already if you've seen or read her plays.

Jane has chosen, herself, not to reveal facts of her life before she became a writer. She remains a playwright without a past, a kind of woman without a country—not unlike so many of the pioneers who settled Kentucky from older states like North Carolina, Virginia, and Pennsylvania. Many of those brave hunters and settlers came into this New Eden and for a variety of reasons changed their names and took on new identities. Simon Kenton, that icon of early Kentucky history, became Simon Butler when he arrived from Virginia in 1775 believing (mistakenly) that he had fatally injured a rival for a young lady's affections. Eventually, he revealed his true identity, but I doubt if Jane Martin ever will. Since she chooses to remain an enigma, I'll have to continue to speak for her.

I can also tell you that Jane has a kitchen. Indeed, she has delivered a number of her manuscripts to me at her kitchen table; but, alas, she has never served me any of her home cooking. Perhaps under her real name she cooks up fabulous Kentucky foods—from burgoo to chess pie—and serves mint juleps on Derby Day to dozens of her friends and family. That part of her life, however, is a door closed to the public. I can tell you that Jane is not overly fleshy, despite her fondness for fast food. Her fondness for food-on-the-fly should be obvious to her fans. She has enshrined Arby's and McDonald's in a number of her monologues. She has, for example, paid tribute to the ubiquitous golden arches on the American landscape in *French Fries*, featuring one of my favorite of her creations, an elderly lady named Anna Mae, who will walk seven miles to get to her clean, well-lighted feast. It's a place of good food, fun and fellowship, a place where she once witnessed a man "healed by a Big Mac." It's her American Dream. "If I had one wish in my life," she announces, "why, I'd like to live in McDonald's."

Well, so much for my friend and client Jane Martin. She may be a woman without a past, but her representative is not. Indeed, my ancestors were cooking varmint stews over pathside fires along the Wilderness Trail with Daniel Boone and James Harrod while Henry Clay was still nursing his mother's milk back in Virginia. The Shyrocks. They were all my people. Way back before Kentucky became the fifteenth state, Old Solomon Speer was being scalped by an unfriendly Shawnee at his salt-rendering kettles on the Salt River—while his brother Jacob was making whiskey in what is now Bourbon County.

My own family memories of food go back to the early 1950s, and they always remind me of some of my favorite relatives. We were not really poor, but we were Scottish and German and frugal and knew how to stretch a single meal over several days. Sunday dinner often featured my mother's baked leg of lamb with mint jelly and roasted potatoes, carrots, fresh peas, mushrooms, and onions. Ah, I can still smell the aroma and taste the succulent meat and vegetables. But that leg of lamb had an awesome longevity. After skipping one day, we revisited the lamb on Tuesday, this time served sliced and cold and surrounded by baked potatoes and warmed-over peas. My mother was in charge of the lamb's remains until Thursday, when Nana, my Great-Aunt Sarah Burns Scott, who lived with us, took over the surviving lamb and gravy and made lamb stew. Well, that's what she called it. All she had left to work with was a lamb bone with a few pieces of meat still clinging to it and several tablespoons of gravy. Nana removed the shreds of meat from the bone, which she boiled for hours in a large kettle. Then she added large chunks of potatoes and carrots, several onions cut into quarters, and the remaining meat and gravy. After the mixture was boiled into a watery mass, she poured it into our large tureen and delivered it to the table, where my father ladled it onto our waiting plates. We had to be careful not to tilt our plates or the "stew" would flow out like water. With a weighty piece of bread, however, it made good sopping. Nana beamed over her creation—and indeed it was something of a miracle to see how *much* she could do with so little—but I always thought it looked and tasted more like thin vegetable soup than lamb stew.

Aunt Nana was mistress of the lamb stew, but Aunt Peggy, Margaret Bunting Mills, was equally famous for her molded cranberry jelly. I don't remember that her recipe was unique, but her "presentation" certainly was. She amassed a large collection of old English jelly molds into which she poured her liquefied jelly. The centerpiece of her collection was a lion sitting atop a pile of rocks. When the mixture was jelled and ready to be released from the mold, she was like a highly skilled artist at work. It was a trick I learned at her knee and have never forgotten. First, she pressed down the jelly all around the edge of the mold with her fingers. Next, with her index finger she pulled the jelly away from the edge in several spots to let air into the mold. Then, she inverted the mold onto a dish leaving the jelly standing up in perfect form, like an exquisite carving. It never failed. Alas, Aunt Peggy may have been a whiz at cranberry jelly, but she knew nothing about figuring portions. Invariably, she would prepare one box of frozen peas for dinner, whether she was serving two or twenty-two. There were times when I could count my serving of peas on the fingers of one hand.

Finally, I must tell about one of my life's first great lessons, which I learned at the age of seven from an encounter with two doomed hens and my great-grandmother. First, the moral: Sooner or later, your grandmother will catch you in a lie. Now, the story. Once upon a summer I was living with my Great-Grandmother Marie Pemberton Mills on her farm outside Lexington, Kentucky. My first early morning chore was to feed and water the chickens in the fattening coops next to the carpenter shop in the backyard.

One morning as I was eating breakfast, Grandmother Mills asked me if I'd fed the chickens. I said I had. I lied. A short time later she said, "Now, Sandy, we're going to have baked chicken for dinner, so I want you to take two hens out of the fattening coop, chop off their heads and bring them in to me." It was the first time I'd been given such an important responsibility. I went out to the carpenter shop and carefully selected a small, sharp hatchet that I thought would do the job. I took the hatchet out and laid it on the chopping block, where I'd seen my grandfather cut kindling and my grandmother dispatch chickens. Then I approached the coop to fetch my first victim. I knew it was their nature to peck at hands being thrust into their living space, especially when they were hungry, and I was hesitant. Finally, I collected my nerves, thrust my hand in quickly, grabbed a hen by the legs, and took her squawking to the block. I placed the hen on her side and beheaded the bird with one whack. I watched her flopping headless around on the ground, fascinated that it took her so long to die. Then I turned back to the head on the block and became frightened as the eyes kept opening and closing. But my job was only half done. I went back to the coop, caught the second bird, and dispatched her in the same manner.

When they both quit flopping on the ground, I took them to the kitchen porch where Grandmother was waiting with a large lard can of boiling water in which she scalded the chickens before plucking their feathers. It was a smelly, messy business which I left to Grandmother. She removed the hens from the hot water and pulled their feathers off inside a flour sack. The feathers were saved for use in making pillows. After she had plucked both hens and singed them over a high flame at the kitchen range, it was time for the evisceration to begin. That was the worst part! As a city child I had never watched anyone do it before. At that point in the process, I was quite sure I would never eat a piece of chicken again.

I was about to go out into the yard for some fresh air when my grandmother, standing at the kitchen sink cleaning and cutting the hens with the skill of a master butcher, turned to me suddenly and said, "I thought you said you fed the hens this morning." I froze. How did she know? I said, "Yes, ma'am. I did." Surely two lies were no worse than one. Whereupon Grandmother Mills reached out to me, with chicken entrails in hand, and gave me my first lesson in biology and lying. She said, "Now look here. If you had fed those hens, there would be corn in their craws. Now go and feed the rest of those poor hens in the fattening coop. And don't you ever lie to me again."

Tearfully, I trudged out to the coop, stopping by the chopping block to see if the eyes of the dead hens were still winking at their killer. Mercifully, they weren't. I fed the remaining hens. At least, they would die fat and full. By the time the hens were baked and their delicious smells filled the house, I had forgotten my anxieties. But sometimes I can still see the hens' terrible blinking eyes, which seem to be saying, "You killed us before you even gave us our last meal." I may have been higher on the food chain than they were, but with the aid of my grandmother's sharp hawk eyes, those hens had brought me low.

As a tribute to them, I present below one of my favorite recipes for baked chicken. It's so good it might even lure Jane Martin out of those fast food emporiums.

Grandmother's Baked Chicken

Kill and dress a three-and-one-half- to five-pound hen. Stuff it with your favorite homemade bread or cornbread stuffing. (Pepperidge Farm will do in a pinch.) Truss the hen and rub well over with butter about the size of an egg. Sprinkle liberally with garlic salt and paprika. Place in a roasting pan in a 450-degree oven, uncovered, until brown, which takes about twenty to thirty minutes. Then add one cup chicken stock and cover with the lid of the roasting pan. Reduce heat to 325 degrees and cook for about one hour more, basting frequently until done. More time may be necessary if hen is old and tough. Serve with giblet gravy made with pan drippings and chicken stock.

∽Jane Martin, Kentucky's most famous anonymous playwright, first came to national attention for *Talking With . . .*, a collection of monologues that premiered at Actors Theatre of Louisville in 1981. Since its New York premiere at the Manhattan Theatre Club in 1982, *Talking With . . .* has been performed around the world, winning the premier new play award given by the American Theatre Critics Association and the Best Foreign Play of the Year Award in Germany from *Theater Heute* magazine. Her other work includes *Cementville* (1991 Humana Festival), *Summer* (1984 Shorts Festival), *Vital Signs* (1990 Humana Festival), *Jack and Jill* (1996 Humana Festival), *Middle-aged White Guys* (1995 Humana Festival), and *Kelly and Du*, which premiered in the 1993 Humana Festival and was nominated for the Pulitzer Prize in drama and won, in 1994, the American Theatre Critics Association Award for Best New Play. In 1997 Martin won, for the third time, the American Theatre Critics Association's top new play award for *Jack and Jill*.

⟠Alexander Speer, Actors Theatre of Louisville's Executive Director, has been with ATL for thirty-one years. During his tenure, the theater has grown from a fledgling company operating on a budget of less than $200,000 to a world-renowned theater with a budget in excess of seven million dollars. Speer is responsible for coordinating all the financial affairs of the organization and for serving as liaison between the Board of Directors and the Theatre's administrative staff. Nationally, he has been Treasurer and Executive Committee member of LORT, the League of Resident Theatres that represents the interests of fifty-five non-profit professional theaters, and he serves on the Theatre Advisory Council of the National Corporate Theatre Fund. He is an incorporator, board member, and treasurer of the American Theatre Exchange Initiative, which promotes theatrical exchange between theaters in the United States and the countries of the former Soviet Union. Speer, who attended Centre College, has taught theater management at leading universities and has served as a consultant to theaters around the country.

The Innisfree Rock

MARTHA BENNETT STILES

The dinner my mother served my older sister's thirteenth birthday houseparty guests was a triumph that compensated her anxious, conformist daughters for all the experiments she had dished out to us—and worse, to our guests—ever since our family settled in the country.

My mother was an art student city girl who married a navy man. Everything interested her; she pitied the wives who fretted over the possibility of remote assignments. "If Forrest and I were stationed on Guam," she would say, "I would make an illustrated catalogue of the shells." I write "catalogue" because she would have written "catalogue." She was from Charleston, South Carolina, where *flavor* was spelled "flavour," *gar-*

den was pronounced "gyarden," and "recipe" was not uttered. The word was, and remains, *receipt*.

My father was only thirty-five when the Depression-strapped navy retired him. A farm, he announced, was the place to teach children discipline, industry, and the facts of life. He and my mother bought fifty acres of broomgrass, honeysuckle, and loblolly pine on the banks of Virginia's James River, called it a farm, and named it Innisfree, for the bean rows they planted, the bee-loud apiary they installed, and the river "water lapping with low sounds by their shore." When one of our Saanens freshened late, they named the kid Peace, "for peace comes dropping slow." They read my nine-year-old sister and me "The Lake Isle of Innisfree." We appreciated it, but our classmates called their pets Blackie and Spot and lived on farms named for trees. Our parents were too pleased with themselves to notice our shame.

My mother went after Innisfree's fauna as if it had been the shells of Guam. She packed her bookshelves with guides, from *Edible and Useful Wild Plants of the United States and Canada* to the latest county extension service bulletins. Anne and I learned to gather wild sorrel and, for a penny apiece, puffballs. We were enthusiastic about fried puffballs and steamed wild asparagus, but not about chickweed in our salads. "It is *not* just like grass," my mother protested. "People can't digest grass. Chickweed is digestible and nutritious." Anne and I were nervous about poke greens that, cut a day older, would have been poisonous, but at least they didn't taste exactly like grass.

With our own honey and arduously squeezed juice from the stemmy fruit that lit up our mulberry tree with fireflies, my mother made wine. With moldy-looking Mother of Vinegar and juice from windfall green apples, she made vinegar, then pickled wild garlic buds. Anne and I preferred lemonade and store-bought gherkins.

With the red fruits of the prickly pear cactus that attacked our bare feet, Mother made an amber jam, so glutinous it sheeted in translucent film from any utensil. Tricked finally onto toast, it hung intractably over the edges like a hound dog's lolling tongue. This recalcitrant jam was a treat compared to the sickly sweet preserves, the color and consistency of frogs' eggs, that she made of the lime-shaped passionflower fruit. At first Anne and I had gathered these "Maypops" joyfully, because, given toothpicks for legs, they made pigs. After one exposure to those preserves, we regarded passionflower fruits with horror. "There's a Maypop," my father would cry: "Step on it before your mother makes preserves!" We didn't step; we jumped, with both feet.

My father missed Anne's thirteenth birthday. With the country at war, he was again on active duty. His absence was probably the reason Anne was able to extract the promise from Mother that no one at her house party was to be served milk. My father was on our side about May-pops, but he took a sadistic delight in serving goat's milk to everyone who came to Innisfree, especially his daughters' appalled teachers. Mother's promise encouraged Anne and me to hope for the best.

Anne's friends swam happily all morning, ate nice, safe, store-bought hot dogs for lunch, and swam happily all afternoon. Then, one by one, they drifted through the kitchen, scouting out supper. I have Mother's letter to my father describing exactly what she was fixing, and how each girl reacted.

Growing up in Charleston, Mother had not liked fish. "The cook always turned its head toward me," she told us. "Stationed" on a river, she studied cookbooks, from her great-grandmother's *The American Frugal Housewife: Dedicated to Those Who Are Not Ashamed to Practice Economy* to *La Cuisine Francaise*. ("If you must serve leftovers, give them a French name," she advised Anne and me.) Earlier in the morning than the stores opened, she would visit the wharf where the fishermen tied up who sold to the stores. They took to saving anything special for her. One triumph I remember was a pompano. No one but my South Carolina mother had known what it was.

For Anne's birthday, Mother had chosen a Rock.

"Fish? Oh Mrs. Wells, I don't like fish!"

"Mrs. Wells, I can't eat fish!"

"Just give me lots of potatoes, Mrs. Wells; I never eat fish."

Every guest gave the same warning. "Just taste it," my unmoved mother told each one. I was thankful my father wouldn't witness the disaster. I tried to believe that the large birthday cake I knew was hidden somewhere would redeem Anne's day.

Innocent of a musical style still about ten years down the road, my mother called her creation "Innisfree Rock." I will never forget her face as she removed its platter from the dining room, making a place for that cake I'd counted on to console everyone. There wasn't a scrap of fish left.

Next evening, the phone began to ring. "I would eat fish," Anne's friends had gone home and said, "if you would fix it the way Mrs. Wells does." Their mothers bought cloudy-eyed artifacts at the stores and fried them precisely as they fried chicken and pork chops. "Jane," they begged, "tell us what you did!"

She had bought her rock the day it was caught; split it, removed its spine, dusted it with flour and salt, and broiled it brown. Then, while it baked at 325 degrees, she browned its finely chopped liver in sausage drippings. To this she added the roe, hot water, salt, pepper, a tablespoonful of soy sauce, a teaspoonful of her own garlic vinegar, and flour to thicken. She poured this sauce over the rock and sprinkled it with minced fronds of the wild fennel that grew taller than I along the riverbluff. No French name was necessary.

In Charleston, where my mother had gone to private school and debuted at the St. Cecilia Society, my grandmother lamented to her friends, "Jane is pioneering in Virginia!" but my mother sang in her chains by the sea. As for Anne and me, Innisfree has been lost to us for more than forty years, but we hear its waters lapping in the deep heart's core.

∿Martha Bennett Stiles grew up in Virginia, where her grandsire, the subject of her young adult novel, *One Among the Indians*, was a three-year hostage to Powhatan. In 1967, Stiles and her husband bought land in Bourbon County, Kentucky, near where his grandparents began married life. The thoroughbreds they have bred include the 1991 two-year-old filly champion of Canada. Stiles's articles and stories have appeared in *Esquire*, *The Virginia Quarterly Review*, *Georgia Review*, *TriQuarterly*, *Seventeen*, *The Thoroughbred Record*, *Worldview*, *Mankind*, etc. She has taught creative writing at the Universitys of Kentucky and Louisville. Her books for young people include *Sara the Dragon Lady* (New York child moves to Kentucky); *Kate of Still Waters* (Kentucky farm crisis; winner of a Society of Children's Book Writers' award); *The Strange House at Newburyport* (about the Underground Railroad); *Darkness Over the Land* (an ALA notable book about World War II in Munich); *The Star in the Forest* (medieval France); and *Island Magic*, Stiles's third picturebook. Awards have included two Hopwood prizes, a Kentucky Arts Council Professional Assistance Grant, an Al Smith Fellowship, and two Frankfort Arts Foundation fiction prizes.

Guineas and
Griddle Cakes:
Two Kentucky Portraits

RICHARD TAYLOR

An old photograph of Cousin Lucy shows her astride Nell, the pet mare she loved to ride around the farm. In those distant 1930s, the farm consisted of about 140 acres. It was located off Lime Kiln Lane in eastern Jefferson County about eight miles from the Louisville city limits. Wearing a sporty hat whose trimmed-back brim makes it seem somehow a briefer version of a man's, she is in quarter profile, dressed in an old sweater and some sort of riding jumper with buttons both at the neck and at the calves of the billowing leggings. One low-heeled shoe is visible, hooked into the stirrup. A child of this century, she sits the mare like a man, not being content to ride sidesaddle, as was expected of women in her youth. She is in her mid- to late fifties. The face, tilted down toward the reins in her left hand, is mostly shaded, her right hand resting on the pommel. The shadows over her full cheeks and pert, upturned nose mask what seems to be a smile. Behind her is a snarl of branch ends encroaching into a milky sky. Other limbs from a tree in the background seem to rise out of Nell's head almost like antlers, the bit and bridle segmenting the maned neck and upper neck in neat geometrical plats. Long, frazzled wisps of timothy or fescue poke out of the field. Cousin Lucy and Nell dominate the landscape, as they do in memory.

Not pictured is her sister Mony, whose name, rhyming with "Tony," is a homemade diminutive of Edmonia. Edmonia Spurgin. When Cousin Frank snapped the photo of Lucy, Mony was probably in the kitchen. The kitchen was a pretty safe bet, for in kitchens she spent the better part of her life, less by necessity than inclination. The long, narrow room at the back of the house was her uncontested domain where she tirelessly prepared meal after meal, at first for Lucy and her brother Frank, then, after his death, for the two of them. Frank himself, dead before I was born, is a kind of cipher. He owned and operated a small printing company, but the only image I have of him derives from my mother who remembered that both Lucy and Mony doted on him. She can remember him retiring after meals to a maroon leather daybed off the front parlor where he would contentedly smoke his pipe. After Frank's death, they usually sat at the small kitchen table from whose window they could gaze out on the east side of the yard, which was punctuated by shade trees and a row of bridal-wreath spirea against the whitewashed fence that looked out over the pasture.

Neither Cousin Lucy nor Cousin Mony ever married. Unmarried women in their generation were common, as was staying at home to keep house and look after aging parents. Their spinsterhood and the surname Spurgin were among the few characteristics they shared. Though both were ardent teetotalers, I remember Cousin Lucy in her later years sipping a glass or two of sherry at Christmas dinner. Both, it was said discreetly among my father's generation, soured on alcohol because none of their brothers, except Frank, ever "amounted to much." Several of them, I later heard, had drinking problems. Besides Frank, I can name only one—Finas—named because his parents intended him to be the last. But that was before the birth in 1882 of Lucy, who supplanted him as the youngest child. She, Mony, and their four or five brothers had been reared near the small town of Eminence in rural Henry County, Kentucky.

Both were members of the Methodist Church, though by the time I knew them age and distance kept them from attending very often. I have one vivid memory of a pie supper under sugar maples at the plain white church that fronted Old Brownsboro Road. I can remember long tables and folding chairs, and men in their shirtsleeves—old men, most of them, browned and creased from years laboring in the fields. They stood in twos and threes while the women sat in sociable groups, filling their plates only after the men and children had been served. My parents' car, a black 1948 Chevy sedan, was pulled off in the churchyard, its bulbous fenders shining under the trees. I must have been seven or eight. Cousin Lucy herself told me of a wedding supper for one of the daughters of a local farmer at which thirteen of the guests had died of food poisoning from eating some unrefrigerated chicken salad.

I have no other memory of them in church, partially because my father, who was closest to them, almost never went to church, preferring to cultivate the spirit with a hoe in his hand among the splendors of his garden. Partially, too, because age hindered Lucy's ability to drive her reliable Chrysler. Mony herself never sat behind a wheel, never really had the desire to leave the farm. There were afternoons when we all went out to Sunday dinner at the Old Stone Inn in Simpsonville, followed by my father driving them along the backroads that Mony and Lucy had known as productive farms during their girlhoods. Though tobacco and cattle were staples, the chief crop had been potatoes, and nearby St. Matthews during the Twenties styled itself the largest exporter of potatoes in North America, if not the world. As they passed each farm, they commented on the families that had lived there, many of whom had been buried for thirty years. Both, if such a question were not too personal, would profess conventional Protestant beliefs. Though both were very proper, neither was preachy. God was a benevolent absentee proprietor, always acknowledged but seldom mentioned, never a topic of discussion.

They bore little physical resemblance to each other. Lucy was small-boned and squat, but usually animated. With her quick step and the habit of cocking her head to take in the world through clear, square-framed glasses, she exuded vitality and self-confidence. She survived the Depression among the employed as a school principal. Even without that income, one senses that Lucy and Mony could have simply retreated to the farm and sustained themselves as their forebears had, using milk money for their few other necessities. Fueled by some hidden well of nervous energy, Lucy was always in motion. She had a businesslike mien and always looked everyone directly in the eye. She didn't walk, she traveled. My sister Treva described her expression as imperious, but I don't remember the slightest arrogance or harshness. With children, that look—a sternness she must have adopted as a school principal—could be unnerving. My cousin Mary Lawrence describes her admiringly as "one stiff piece of rope." It's true that she had a strong sense of propriety, but she stopped far short of prudishness. I never heard her raise her voice or say a mean-spirited thing. Though she greatly admired both Roosevelts, she was naturally conservative in her view of things, having few good words for the social upheavals that followed the war. She was fit, always seeming much more robust than in fact she was, standing about five foot one or two. The contrast of her pale blue eyes and ruddy complexion gave her a scrubbed and healthy appearance even into her late seventies. Lucy, as the name denotes, was all light and energy. She was her own sun.

Mony, a decade older, was taller but very spare, thin to the point of frailness. She was pale, sometimes even sallow, perhaps because she spent most of her time indoors. Her arms, except when she rolled dough on the marble slab on her kitchen counter, were always sleeved to the wrist, and her dress was always secured at the neck by a clasp or ivory-white cameo. She, like Lucy, wore thick, flesh-colored stockings and cobby shoes with blocked heels. Her simple, high-necked dresses were usually Amish gray or busy prints that resembled the speckled backs of her guinea fowls, birds in which she exhibited the most unapologetic pride. Neither she nor her sister wore skirts—only dresses. And never slacks. Naturally gentle though not genteel, she shunned pretense of any kind. It was true that when she dressed up in dark blue she often wore a lace collar, a carryover from her mother's or grandmother's generation. I never in memory saw Cousin Mony wearing a bright color. Her natural backdrops were kettle gray and spatterware saucepans. Her shoulders were narrow and sharp, her collarbones protruding like folded wings. The skin hung loose on her face, and there was a dewlap under her chin. On the back of her left wrist was a kidney-shaped rust mark. She was, as my father might say, "a gentle soul." Mild and unobtrusive, she wore her wispy dark hair on the back of her head in a modest bun, not so unlike the farm wife of Grant Wood's "American Gothic," who was enough her contemporary to have been a schoolmate. She was covertly hard-working, and in her quiet way had something of Lucy's drive, expending that energy in household chores and at the kitchen range. She was tranquil almost to the point of simpleness, but this was chiefly because she deferred to Lucy, through whose eyes she largely saw the larger world. Lucy's pragmatically conservative opinions were Mony's opinions though she seldom voiced them, content to let Lucy step forward as her proxy. In the outside world of politics, entertainment, and international affairs, she had little knowledge or interest. In her deference to her younger sister, in her incessant activity and preoccupation with the practical details of daily existence, she was a throwback to the frontier, the rugged farming culture that she had been born to just seven years after the Civil War. She, unlike her sister, was very much at home in the nineteenth century and a little disoriented in this.

Outside the kitchen, her greatest interest lay in poultry, a vital link in the chain from production to consumption, what today we describe as a renewable resource. She and Lucy kept a sizable flock of White Rocks and Rhode Island Reds as well as a few paisley-backed Domineckers. Each morning she would gather eggs from the henhouse, a small building next to the toolshed, whose flat surfaces were always floured with lime, giving the air a pungent chalky smell. To protect her pale skin and eyes when she was outside, she always wore a bonnet. From her bunched apron at feeding time she dispensed handfuls of shelled corn, summoning her chickens in an urgent, high-pitched mewing, "Here chick, chick, chick. Here chick, here." I have seen her shoo an aggressive rooster with a broom, indelicately swatting or even kicking it to underscore the message. From all quarters fat pullets would rush to her, greedily pecking kernels from the grassless chickenyard. They would also eat from her hand, cocking their heads sideways to glare with one appraising eye before gingerly nipping the proferred gold. From these same plump layers each week she would select a candidate for the table. On the appointed day, C.W., their tenant and the only man on the farm, would wring its neck, and she would pluck and dress it herself as a preliminary to the oven or skillet. Promptly at noon it would arrive for Sunday dinner in golden splendor on a platter.

But it was to the guineas—the speckled fowl that originated in West Africa—that she was most attached. My father described them as the wildest and most flavorful of so-called domesticated birds because of their slightly gamy taste. He claimed that guinea cocks were the best eating birds, their dark meat the most succulent of all fowl, wild or domestic. And Cousin Mony not only shared this opinion but greatly abetted him in forming it. Despite the caterwauling of the guineas whenever someone drove up the gravel drive or when they were disturbed at night, she kept as many as two dozen, housing them in a large chicken-wire cage attached to the corncrib in the backyard. This wired enclosure was built several feet off the ground as a check against predators: the usual rogues' gallery of possums, raccoons, weasels, and even the odd fox.

"Oh, they're better than watchdogs," Lucy liked to say. "They racket whenever anything comes into the yard."

As children, my brother, sister, and I were all attracted to what made the boldest appearance or, in this instance, the most raucous noise. We became students of guineas. As they ranged, we noted that they always followed a leader. The hens were so stupid they often led their keets through wet grass where some would be lost while others succumbed to the chills that such forays were said to bring on. When tromping about the yard, they moved, my father used to say, "like a gaggle of nuns," hunched over and a little furtive in their motions. Cousin Mony's attraction went further. In her workaday world, speckled print dresses sewn from flour sacks, she unconsciously flattered them by imitation. They were her totem. And, like them, she went her own way without much troubling anybody else.

Ten years younger and of a different generation, Cousin Lucy had a different temperament. Deciding to become a teacher, she had gone off to Columbia University before the First War and earned both undergraduate and master's degrees in education. She had taught for a time before discovering her knack for administration. For several decades she was the principal of Cochran Elementary, the prestigious public school to which children of prominent downtown families sent their children in preparation for Louisville Male High. She was also a canny businesswoman, eventually owning a downtown parking garage and a quantity of blue-chip stock. As for their speech, they both said "commence" for "start" and would do things "directly." They both pronounced "about" as "aboot," probably a carryover from the speech of their Virginia forebears. Living and working together virtually their entire lives, they formed a composite of home and career—one an industrious but demurring homebody, the other an entrepreneur; one with one foot in the nineteenth century mold of domesticity, the other striding confidently toward the liberated future that beckoned a generation of resourceful and competitive women.

My father, raised on a farm himself and a lifelong student of horticulture, kept his own large garden on the farm and maintained the adjoining orchard as well. In addition to the usual tomatoes, potatoes, okra, rhubarb, and onions, he had an almost obsessive fondness for berries: raspberries, currants, strawberries, gooseberries, and several old-fashioned varieties of grapes. Not content with berries he could grow himself, he and Uncle Lawrence would go on blackberry-picking forays to undisclosed locations, bringing home gallons in a galvanized washtub. At midsummer when the vegetables came in, he would load up the jeep with baskets and distribute mounds of tomatoes, squash, and ears of Silver Queen to city neighbors—the produce coming in successive waves. They thought him a garden prince. He brought my mother bucketfuls of snapdragons, bleeding hearts, coral bells, and antique columbines. When friends had parties, he would bestow this floral plenty on them. Spotting a bush of yellow roses in someone's yard one day, an old-fashioned variety he remembered from childhood, he stopped and asked the owners for a slip and successfully introduced it to his own garden. Whenever he could get away from the law office, he quick-changed into his army-surplus khakis, hopped into his mud-colored '44 Willys, and was off to "the country." This included almost every summer evening and weekend. As often as he could entice or dragoon us, my brother or I would go along, and some of the best hours of my childhood were spent wading in the branch, jumping from the barn loft into manure piles, or building "forts" out of cane and branches among the lichen-blotched boulders on the back half of the farm.

He felt a special affinity for Cousin Mony and Cousin Lucy. They were living connections with the rural ways he'd given up for a career in the city. Though he would never say so, he regarded himself as their protector. After each work session in the garden, he would look in on them. They loved to fuss over him, and we seldom got away without a snack of some kind, biscuits wrapped in a napkin or cold lemonade carried out to the garden where he would be hoeing, weeding, tying up beans, or scrunched up under the temperamental old Gravely mower that he used around the fencerows. They called him by his nickname, which appropriately was Buzz.

Cousin Lucy and Cousin Mony had their own garden, a fenced, half-acre plot twenty-five yards or so from the kitchen door. Next to the garden gate was a work bell, its considerable bulk and weight ingeniously balanced on a single four-by-four post. "Never ring the bell," Cousin Lucy cautioned us, "because in the country ringing the bell is the signal for fire or distress." As the season progressed, Lucy and Mony both bent their backs in the long rows—planting, watering, weeding, and harvesting. Hauling water involved toting buckets from the pump which stood next to the house, nearly thirty yards from the garden gate. When the canning began, the kitchen was converted into a mini-factory, filled with glass mason jars and lids that popped as they cooled on the crowded counter.

They could not have succeeded in the garden without the help of C.W., their black tenant, a burly, thick-shouldered man, in his thirties then, who lived with his family in a modest one-story cottage just to the south of their farmhouse and close by the stockbarn and one-room milkhouse. He ran the dairy and did practically all of the heavy work on the whole farm. His name was C.W. Davis, though he was always known simply as C.W. After Frank's death, and probably before, he worked under the watchful tutelage of Cousin Lucy. She called him C.W.; he always referred to her as "Miss Lucy." Though I didn't think anything of it then, he was the first person of color I'd ever known. C.W. was a willing worker. He had a mild manner and a natural dignity. I never saw him angry, never heard him raise his voice except to stir one of the horses or chase a stray cow from the garden. He was a great favorite of my brother and me because he sometimes let us ride on the Farm-All with him or on the utility wagon when there was baled hay, fallen limbs, or manure to haul. Each spring, once the ground had dried sufficiently, C.W. would plow and disc the garden plot. Attaching a plow to the Farm-All, he would turn up the soil, leaving rows of darkly glazed furrows where the silver share had sliced.

It was no secret that Cousin Mony loved to cook. Preparing food was her art, her passion, the thing she could do best and from which she derived the most satisfaction and much justified praise. Though she was more than a fair hand at needlework and could sew with consummate skill, the allure of concocting a blackberry cobbler or frying a chicken with dumplings was more immediately rewarding. Unlike most cooks I've encountered, she was a light eater. Like most of those who were accomplished, she followed fixed procedures. For instance, after every meal, she re-set the table, placing plates and silverware as well as condiments on the small kitchen table or the "company" table in the dining room that adjoined the kitchen. This was not so unusual in itself, but she would cover the table with a second tablecloth, producing a white expanse of steeples and cones that resembled an imaginary snowscape in the Swiss Alps. Whether she did this to protect the dishware from houseflies or through some exaggerated sense of cleanliness, I don't know, but it was her undisputed way. It may have been a habit picked up from her own mother. A second was keeping the kitchen scrupulously clean, washing or wiping off in stages even while the meal was being prepared.

What was the connection between them and my father? We were blood relations through their mother Susan Spurgin, whose maiden name had been Susan Barrick, one of three daughters of a farming family that lived in then-rural Oldham County. Her sister, Edmonia Barrick, had been the second wife of my great-grandfather, Philip Richard Taylor, who had married Edmonia in the early 1860s. Both Cousin Lucy and Cousin Mony called me Dick, sometimes mentioning my grandfather's brother Dick— "Uncle Dick," my father called him—who had been a great favorite of Lucy's and Mony's generation.

Several family stories about Mony's kitchen have come down to us. I can vividly remember the antiquated, wood-fired, cast-iron kitchen range that dominated one wall of her kitchen. It was Mony's altar, which she tended with great devotion. Next to it was a bucket always filled with kindling, and its ashes were carried out to what now is called a compost pile. Since the cookstove had no controls or gauges, she kept an even heat by lifting from time to time one of the metal plates on the stove top to inspect the fire. The handle of her lifting piece had coils of springs around it to absorb the heat. Lifting the plates, she had an intuitive sense of how much heat the fire was producing and could add more wood or turn down the damper on the stovepipe according to her needs. She simply passed her hand over the opening and knew precisely what to do. In the commodious compartment next to the firebox she did her baking.

One Christmas, Cousin Lucy, thinking that she could lighten Mony's kitchen burdens and simultaneously introduce her to twentieth-century technology, bought a state-of-the-art General Electric stove, a white-enameled beauty with dials and knobs enough to satisfy the most fastidious chef. Cousin Mony thanked Lucy for her thoughtfulness and said that she might still need her old stove for dishes that were especially ticklish. So the two stoves sat side by side in the kitchen, the one gleaming and unused, the other an anachronistic quarter ton of cast iron whose finish resembled unpolished gun metal. Despite the labor-saving efficiency of the new range, it became obvious that she preferred the relic, which she kept reliably stoked with wood and performing in the old way. After a week or so when it was clear that Mony hadn't so much as heated water on the new stove, Lucy asked why. Mony's response was that she knew it wouldn't heat properly, that it wasn't as predictable or efficient as her beloved wood-burner. Perhaps it was as much a matter of time. Mony knew how to pace herself on the woodstove, which demanded almost constant attention. This new appliance saved her too much time. Cousin Lucy finally removed it and gave it to C.W., and so restored the kitchen to its nineteenth-century purity.

The second story is by way of apologizing for not including the recipe of the dish it describes. On nearly every Saturday or Sunday morning my father managed to find himself at the farm. When frost took the garden, he simply changed venues. During the winter months he would recruit several of us and go out to the rough, wooded slopes at the back of the farm to search for black locust, the hardwood he regarded as the best-burning. Despite the nuisance of thorns on its ropy bark, its density and heat value were unsurpassed; its straight-grained yellowish wood split easily. At other times we gathered walnuts, especially prolific on the big tree that stood on the edge of the woods in the lower pasture below the stockbarn. Wearing rubber gloves to mitigate staining, using wooden mallets to split the lime-green hulls, a gang of us would fill a half-dozen bushel baskets and put them somewhere to season and dry for eating later. Many must have been grated into Cousin Mony's pies and salads.

Invariably, we were invited to have "a little something" for breakfast. One principle that Cousin Mony and Cousin Lucy both shared was an insistent hospitality that bordered on the militant. It was unthinkable for anyone to leave the premises without taking in a few calories. Just as in the Civil War when what began as a skirmish often heated up as a battle, in Cousin Mony's kitchen what began as a snack would quickly take on the dimensions of a meal. She liked to feed people, especially men, whose job it was on the farm to do work that was best done on a full stomach. Both Lucy and Mony praised appetites and were a little distrustful of light eaters. Simply stepping into a kitchen merited, at the very least, a steaming biscuit loaded with butter and grape jelly.

"Eat up," Cousin Lucy would say. "You look a little puny today." My father was particularly partial to Cousin Mony's hot water cornbread, a fried-in-bacon-grease griddle cake which is a German cousin to the conventional pancake. So taken was he with this dish that he deputized my older teenage sister Treva to visit Cousin Mony expressly to witness its preparation. Her charge was to bring the recipe home. All that was known beforehand was that water was used to mix the ingredients instead of milk. She did visit, but her mission failed.

"And how much butter do you add?" she would ask.

"Just a little," said Mony.

Everything—bacon grease, eggs, or flour—was a pinch of this, a handful of that. "Mix in some sugar," she would say, dolloping an indeterminate amount into the stoneware mixing bowl. Never three teaspoons or a quarter of a cup—nothing so precise. The amounts were not exact because Mony measured from experience of eye and taste rather than by numbers or print on the page. She did own a battered old cookbook, but it consisted mostly of recipes exchanged with friends or cut out from newspapers and paperclipped to the pages. Most of her recipes she carried in her head, and most of her art, unfortunately, went with her when she died. So my father was frustrated in his effort to get a recipe for hot water griddle cakes at home, but that didn't deter him from enjoying them at the small, oilcloth-covered table in her kitchen.

In addition to chickens and the occasional guinea, she cooked veal and leg of mutton, sometimes a roast beef. In the spring she had us gather watercress from a wet, low area by the branch that meandered across the pasture. Washed and seasoned with a little salt and vinegar, it made a delicious salad. She baked more biscuits than bread, though cornbread was also a regular. My mother remembers that for supper Mony routinely served two kinds of potatoes, usually boiled Idaho potatoes and yams. She was famed for her desserts, especially her blackberry cobblers and the meringue that she served frozen with layers of raspberry sherbet. During the summer months she always kept a pitcher of ice-cold water in the refrigerator. I can remember the chill beads on the glasses when it was poured. In the garden there was always a plot devoted to melons, and I can vividly reconstruct the green vines snaking from the mounds, the flowering tendrils ballooning into muskmelons, watermelon, and cantaloupes. The following is a recipe for watermelon pickles, belonging to Cousin Mony and resurrected from my mother's store of time-tried favorites:

Watermelon Pickles

Select four pounds from rind of melon and cut in one-inch cubes. Weigh before putting in lime water. Soak two and one-half hours in lime water. Dry well, cover with fresh water, and let stand overnight. Drain next morning. Cover with fresh water and boil two and one-half hours until tender, adding water if necessary, if it boils dry.

Lime Water Brine
two quarts cold water
two tablespoons lime (purchase in drugstore)

Vinegar Syrup
two quarts vinegar
one pint water
four and one-half cups sugar
two tablespoons allspice
two tablespoons cloves
ten small cinnamon sticks

Bring syrup to boil, add rind and boil two hours until syrup thickens. Pack in sterile jars, seal, and keep in a cool place. These are crisp and delicious. The main problem is finding a watermelon with a thick, white rind.

The succession of meals would have gone on indefinitely had not the century finally caught up with them. When Mony entered her eighties, they both knew it was time to move to town. Mony had broken her hip in a fall, and afterwards had trouble getting around. Though she would never confess it, she was in pain. She effectively hid her stiffness and altered gait, but there were other signs. Her meals became less elaborate; her cooking for company, less frequent. Finally, Lucy bought a lot in St. Matthews and built a comfortable brick house to her specifications. They got on pretty well, though Mony's woodstove had been a casualty of the move and was left behind. By way of explanation, Lucy concocted several alternate excuses, namely city ordinances and fire insurance regulations. Storing and toting the firewood would also be a problem. The truth was that Mony was tired, and C.W. was no longer around to help since he and his family had moved to downtown Louisville where for a time he managed Cousin Lucy's parking garage.

The farm was sold to developers, who soon dismantled most of the farming operation and converted the rolling fields into a suburban enclave. I can remember as a kid chasing rabbits in the front field behind a hay cutter while grownups pitched square bales on the bed of a wagon. Now that field is a gridwork of barn-sized brick houses with black, oversized mailboxes and manicured yards supporting exotic flora watered by elaborate sprays piped from the city reservoir. Neither Mony nor Lucy, so far as I know, returned to see the transformation. Neither, I suspect, had the heart to.

∿Richard Taylor is a professor of English at Kentucky State University in Frankfort, Kentucky. Having grown up in Louisville, he holds a Ph.D. in English from the University of Kentucky and a J.D. from the University of Louisville. He has published a novel (*Girty*, Gnomon Press), two collections of poems (*Bluegrass* and *Earthbones*, Larkspur Press and Gnomon), and *Three Kentucky Tragedies*, a part of the new readers series published by University Press of Kentucky. He has won two creative writing fellowships from the National Endowment for the Arts and an Al Smith Fellowship in Creative Writing from the Kentucky Arts Council. A former dean and teacher in the Governor's Scholars Program, he received the Distinguished Professor Award at K.S.U. in 1992. He and his wife live near Frankfort with their three children and own Poor Richard's Books in historic downtown Frankfort.

Merchants of Christmas

GERALD TONER

No right-minded American would stand up for the proposition of a commercialized Christmas. Commercialism at Christmas is everyone's favorite whipping boy and understandably so. During Christmas our emotions are such a mess that we hardly need another weepy Hallmark spot or the stress of beating your sister-in-law to the last Tickle Me Elmo. Moonlight Madness sales eat up our holiday evenings, and Budweiser semis keep their appointed rounds in our late nights before the television.

Common sense, however, never prevents us from getting caught up in the rush and forgetting the purpose of our gifts. A mere handful of laudable zealots resist the retail frenzy that haunts us from sometime shortly after Halloween until the stroke of midnight Christmas Eve. Most of us fall lemming-like into line, get all caught up with the insanity, and end up feeling just a little guilty by Christmas Day. "Alas, we fell for the commercial bait again!"

Take heart. I dedicate this brief reminiscence to the hapless majority who from year to year break their resolve from the year before and break their necks shopping until they drop. At least in a limited sense, I hereby attest to the uplift brought on by a shopping spree or two: for me, the American retail tradition helped bridge the emotional void created by my mother's sudden death.

By Thanksgiving of 1960 my grandmother was still coping with the death of her only child and the failing health of her second husband. My father, an old-school stoic, held his feelings to himself while doing his best to take over as a single parent years before single parenting was common. My sister was twenty-one, soon to be engaged, and trying to finish her senior year at the University of Kentucky without totally sacrificing the joys of her first three years of college. Like my father and grandmother, she was also confronted with the problem of a certain ten-year-old boy who had awakened one morning absent a mother. While I alternately presented a poignant problem or a beloved problem or "no problem at all," I nevertheless remained a kid facing a very different Christmas than I'd experienced the year before. My sister was an older kid doing the same.

As Thanksgiving neared, I sensed this difference. Everyone sensed it, though my sister must have realized this earlier than my father or my grandmother. My father had never been an eager Christmas shopper and was less so that year. Grandma had taken over daily duties including cooking, laundry, and making sure that I was transported to the right place at the right time. Like my father, she had lost a life companion. Her once-joy-filled shopping ventures with my mother were things of the past, and thus Christmas traditions were left to my sister and me.

That December we could have undertaken service to the church or helped in soup kitchens or raised money for worthy causes. Perhaps we should have. We didn't. Instead, we became a Santa Claus partnership, dedicated to shopping for each other and everyone else in the family. It was one clear way in which my sister could take charge at a time in our lives and at a time of the year when someone clearly needed to assume control. So she took on the assignment of Christmas and made me, already her needy charge, her faithful assistant as well.

Like a modern and citified Buddy and his "friend" from Truman Capote's *A Christmas Memory*, my sister and I met and conspired to keep alive the spirit of Christmas as it had existed at 543 Highland Avenue—a live tree with big old bulbs and my mother's silver glass ornaments from the year before, adult gifts to be exchanged on Christmas Eve and Santa Claus to arrive on Christmas morning: simple props for the smiles, the words of thanks, the hugs and the kisses that proved hard to come by that Christmas. Unlike Capote's characters, we weren't gathering pecans for fruitcakes nor were we using an old baby buggy to transport our goods. Those first years following mother's death, we made do with a classic 1956 Ford Fairlane convertible and, in later years, my sister's little white Renault.

Sometimes we shopped on Thursday nights, but more often than not, when the weekend approached and the unique, exciting dusk of Friday afternoons in December settled over the Ohio Valley, my sister would gather her little brother under her broad wing and we would set off on a shopping adventure. Whether clear and cold, or overcast and damp (it never snowed before Christmas), Fridays were Christmas time. We must have missed a Friday or two, but my memory has become my history. And my memory is that we piled into the car after my Grandma fed us, then charged off into the night. We cranked up the heater and the radio and rambled off to the retail mecca of Cincinnati.

Expressways had not yet raped the landscape. Today a similar shopping trip would amount to jumping on an exit and being in downtown in five minutes or less. Not back then. The way to the river began by winding through and out of Fort Thomas, out of the northern Kentucky hills once known as the Highlands, through the brief stretch of woods that still separates Fort Thomas from the river towns of an earlier century, Bellevue and Newport, and then into Newport itself. In the dark of early December nights, homes decorated in outdoor lights set the mood for Christmas and offered up fodder for our praise and our sarcasm.

The whole idea of stringing outdoor lights was foreign to our experience. We had never done it! Not that lights were terribly expensive, although that was probably one factor running through my Dad's mind. The prime reason was simply the hassle of putting them up and taking them down a month later. My Dad was a "simplify, simplify, simplify" guy long before it was popular. But if we didn't have our own outdoor lights, my sister and I still enjoyed gawking at everyone else's. We were merciless in our comments: "Too little . . . Too much . . . Just right . . . Spectacular," with no mind whatsoever to our lack of standing to talk.

There was one enterprising realtor in town whom I always assessed as about the richest person in the world based upon the grandiloquence of her yard each Christmas. I had absolutely no reason to know who really was the wealthiest person in Fort Thomas, but my assumption was that it had to be whoever put up the most lights and decorated with the most reindeer, sleighs, and Santas. She certainly did that, but that's a story for another day.

Once out of the sheltered confines of Fort Thomas we entered Newport, sin city of the greater western hemisphere. Still a significant city by Kentucky standards, with a thriving downtown dependent upon all sorts of illicit activities to prime its economic pump, Newport was like a madam from some turn-of-the-century cathouse. Simultaneously grand and shabby, its main thoroughfare, Monmouth Street, was dotted with retail stores and restaurants that would be memories in just ten years. Red, green, blue, and white lights intertwined with sparkling aluminum garlands, criss-crossing Monmouth in a giddy array. Every other block or so there were plastic reindeer and laughing Santa heads on Newport's paint-peeled light poles.

In ten short blocks Monmouth Street yielded to the Central (a left turn) and L & N (a right turn) Bridges over the Ohio. We alternated routes at random since both bridges looked as if they might pitch into the river given a healthy breeze. Both offered imagined risks necessary to make the adventure more fun. We bombed into Cincinnati with the canvas top on the Fairlane vibrating in the rushing wind, our radio turned up to overcome the constant brrrrrrrrr of the windblown top. Our unspoken shopping protocol required parking near Shillito's (now Lazarus) and working our way by foot back into the heart of the merchant district.

In one sense we represented the retailers' dream. First, we liked shopping. Second, the word "SALE" posted on any table was justification for us to stop and assess the treasures being offered up. We meandered through almost every department on Shillito's first floor, theoretically taking the shortest course between our parked car and the next store on the way. While a little threadbare by comparison to Pogue's or Cincinnati's boutique shops clustered on Fourth Street, Shillito's couldn't be beat for specials on leather gloves or manicure sets or shoe shine kits, presents perfect for a ten-year-old's budget. It was a little like wolfing down a

Snicker's bar knowing that Godiva is about to be politely served: we knew we shouldn't, but we did anyway.

After feasting on Shillito's first-floor bargains, we criss-crossed our way through the streets and alleys into Mabley & Carew—usually just a conduit to Pogue's. There was an occasional find in women's slippers or gowns, and once or twice some nice sweaters in the men's department, but usually it was just a comfortable detour to stay warm on a cold night.

Connected on either side of the massive Carew Tower by an arcade, Pogue's (the ultimate stop) looked and smelled and acted like a supporting player out of *Miracle on 34th Street*. Pogue's ceilings were higher, its supporting pillars grander, its displays more elegant, its tea room's milk shakes thicker, its men's department more distinguished, its women's department more sophisticated than any of Cincinnati's other department stores. For all of this hype, Shillito's probably saw more of our dollars, but the fun was in shopping at Pogue's. We fingered the merchandise, checked the prices against those we'd seen elsewhere, asked the over-made-up ladies at the perfume counters for samples, and generally soaked up the ambiance in deep breaths and eyefuls.

I have to admit that the four or five Christmases we followed the routine of Friday night Christmas shopping tend to blur in my mind's eye, and I know that it was later than that first Christmas when the sale of sales arose, but I remember distinctly the sale itself. It involved a table full of men's Daniel Green leather slippers at an unbelievable, once-in-a-lifetime price. We must have stockpiled six pairs and I know they got us through more than one Christmas. Any true shopping addict has experienced the quasi-religious experience of which I speak. Everyone was at the table, trying to eyeball, grab, cajole, and snatch as politely as possible without starting a riot or missing an opportunity. I was in there pushing and shoving with the best of them. When we finished we took a deep breath and laughed ourselves and our bags of shoeboxes back to the car and home, triumphant.

The modern irony of our downtown pilgrimage was that we seldom deigned to cross Fourth Street to shop at McAlpin's, the then-fourth remaining department store in downtown Cincinnati. (Alms and Doepke had closed years before.) After the palatial experience of Pogue's, the practical linoleum floors and fluorescent lighting of McAlpin's seemed far too gauche for two such skilled merchants of Christmas as my sister and me. Yet it is McAlpin's alone that survived the hard-hearted eighties. The others all perished, like dinosaurs in a haze of meteoric dust.

So went our forays into the heart of the shopping district surrounding Fountain Square. More often than not, however, our evening would not end at the big department stores, but at the only mail order retail-discounter I knew in Cincinnati at the time: Richter & Phillips. R & P long preceded Service Merchandise or Circuit City or Wal-Mart or K-Mart or any other "mart." At least as I recall it in the sixties, there were department stores and Mom-and-Pop retailers and very little in between. We didn't realize at the time that we were discount pioneers leading the way to the extinction of downtown shopping as we loved it. We were simply doing our best on a pretty tight budget. Such is America.

R & P was located in an old office building seven or eight floors up. It was plain vanilla, starkly adorned with little or no floor space. After we exited the old, operator-driven elevator, I remember my sister approaching the first employee she came to with a request to see the manager. His name was Fred and my sister knew him through some friend of a friend. With all of her bargain hunter's soul she believed that she could drive the best price by dealing directly with Fred. She was right, of course. We did not grow up "poor," and we certainly weren't "rich," but we grew up with adults who passed on to us their knowledge of how to squeeze a nickel to its best and fullest use.

Fred would emerge from the remote and secret recesses of the "back" and with a weary smile greet my sister and her little brother. Today, "discount" implies an impersonal demeanor, a voiced disinterest, and a certain impatience on the part of the employee unfortunate enough to wait on the public. Admittedly Fred was the owner or the son of the owner, but he exuded anything but disdain. He was a person—a blush-cheeked, strawberry-blond, ruddy-complected human being. In my ten-year-old naiveté, I probably overlooked another element in the equation. My sister was a participant in and winner of more than a few beauty contests. This fact may have escaped her ten-year-old brother, but it didn't elude Fred.

My sister could drive a bargain like no one since the Dutch haggled with shells over Manhattan. She would agonize (always a Tony Award winning performance) over a set of cuff links or a jewelry box for Grandma or a watch for me (to be given as a gift from Grandma). A thirty-five-dollar catalog price quickly became thirty-two fifty or less. My sister was never harsh nor the least bit difficult, but she was never so happy as when she saved another dollar or two off the discounted catalog price. She charmed and cajoled bargains out of store clerks all over the city.

It has also occurred to me, in reflection, that seasoned pros like

Fred knew exactly what was transpiring—much to his delight. He certainly seemed to enjoy it as much as we did. Once the purchase was made, no one departed unhappy. R & P needed the business and my sister and I needed to fill out the remainder of our Christmas list.

Finished at R & P, we would pack ourselves into the car and head for home, our radio louder than on the way over, our voices blending in (sort of) with those of Bing Crosby, Johnny Mathis, Andy Williams, and whatever more secular singers were hot on the Top Forty. Sometimes as we drove we shared a quarter's worth (about a quarter pound) of malted milk balls purchased at a dime store on Race Street between Shillito's and Mabley & Carew. Ignorant of the effect the sugar, fat, and cholesterol were wreaking on our concert-quality voices, we sang and ate with reckless abandon.

To our backs the bright lights of the still-old-fashioned, dowager Queen City burned brightly in the December night. Fountain Square seemed quaint and just a little seedy back then, hardly the spectacle of later years. The riverfront was still dotted with wharfs and barges, and the interstate would not come slashing through for several years. Staring back as we crossed the L & N bridge into Newport, I was always awed by the seeming immensity of Cincinnati's three skyscrapers standing as stolid reminders that I had been shopping in the Big City. Buying and selling in the name of Christ, my sister and I knew that we were doing something still more important—at least on a personal level.

Sometimes we would go back to my grandmother's house and, over cookies and hot chocolate or milk, recount our adventures "over town." Grandma listened, happy for us even when she couldn't yet be settled in the season. By the next year, after my sister married, we would often end up after Cincinnati adventures at her apartment to examine our loot— i.e., other people's soon-to-be-loot—and listen to her exhaustive collection of Christmas music: Frank Sinatra, Nat King Cole, Doris Day, and the Harry Simeone Chorale. Often we'd stay up late and watch the *Tonight Show* or an old movie, though old movies were usually a ritual shared between my father and me. When you add them all up, there weren't more than a dozen of those Friday nights in all, but such evenings remained special because they created a new tradition from the ashes of Christmases past.

Our job was to keep Christmas going at a time when no one was ready for singing carols around a piano that only my mother knew how to play or attending Advent Christmas services or focusing on Christmas traditions past. If we had tried to do these things we would have failed.

I don't remember everything about that first Christmas Eve without my mother, but I do remember one event distinctly. On one of our Friday night forays to R & P my sister and I had purchased (with her money, of course) a punch bowl and cups for my grandmother. Somehow, while I kept Grandma preoccupied in the living room, not ten feet from the dining room table, my sister set out the punch bowl and cups. Then, on signal, I led Grandma, who was a very spry sixty-eight years old, into the dining room. My sister flipped on the lights and my sister and I both cried out "surprise!"

At age ten I probably didn't expect any particular response, but Grandma immediately burst into tears and exited the room. Dumbfounded, I really didn't know what to think. To this day I'm not sure what emotions must have rushed through her. Surely sadness at the sudden reminder of her daughter's death accompanied, perhaps, by some immediate reflections on Christmases past and irretrievable. But I can't help but think that intermixed with her bitter tears of sadness and regret were some somber, guarded, but very real tears of joy—joy that sprang from her realization that the Christmas spirit would continue into another generation.

Grandma loved that punch bowl set, using it often and displaying it proudly on her sideboard or dining room table. It was not a symbol of endings but of beginnings. It was part of a new and inevitable era, a reminder that, whether we liked it or not, life would plug along and new generations would assume control.

Now, obviously, the punch bowl and its cups—like any store-purchased gift—was merely a device. Some gifts are remembered for generations, some are returned the day after Christmas, and some just fade into the odd compilation of stuff we gather throughout our lives until some ultimate garage sale. They are just things. But this gift sprang from the camaraderie of her granddaughter and her ten-year-old grandson, joined together on Friday nights in the hustle and bustle of other strangers on the streets and sidewalks of downtown Cincinnati, and in the crowded aisles and escalators of its once-prosperous, once-magnificent department stores.

Now that some thirty-six years have passed and my saint-like grandmother and my hard working, laconic father are also gone, my sister is guardian over the punch bowl, which when last I visited was put to good use, serving up a 7UP-and-sherbet punch fit for a Baptist wedding reception. She surely remembers Grandma's reaction to our gift and must think of it every time she fills the bowl. Employing greater skill than either my mother or grandmother ever exhibited in the kitchen, she surrounds the bowl's base with a sprinkling of homemade cookies and candies, my favorite of which are her "buckeyes"—chocolate covered peanut butter balls reminiscent of a Reese's Cup made especially for a merchant of Christmas! The recipe is as follows:

Buckeyes

Melt in saucepan: one and one-fourth cups (two and one-half sticks) whipped butter or margarine. Remove from heat. Stir in (do not use mixer): one (sixteen-ounce) box confectioners' sugar and eight ounces smooth peanut butter. Using hands, shape into balls. Combine in saucepan: one (eight ounce) package chocolate chips and one-half stick paraffin. Cook over low heat, stirring constantly, until completely melted. Use toothpick or two-prong fork and dip balls into mixture leaving a small, circular portion uncovered. Let stand on waxed paper until set.

ᕲᕰGerald Toner, who was born and raised in Fort Thomas, Kentucky, earned his A.B. from Harvard College and his J.D. from Vanderbilt University College of Law. He currently lives with his wife and children in Louisville, Kentucky, where he is a partner in the law firm of O'Bryan, Brown & Toner. In addition to his appointment as the first editor-in-chief of the *Kentucky Bar News* newspaper and to serving on the editorial board of *Kentucky Bench & Bar*, Toner's literary career has included publishing numerous short stories in such magazines as *The Saturday Evening Post, Redbook,* and *Ladies Home Journal.* His books include *Lipstick Like Lindsay's and Other Christmas Stories, Whittlesworth Comes To Christmas,* and *Holly Day's Cafe and Other Christmas Stories.* Toner's play, *Wenceslaus,* and his radio play, *The Christmas Visitation,* have been produced at the Kentucky Center for the Arts.

Sweet Cobblers and Stack Cakes

Shirley Williams

In 1994, three friends and I put together an oral history play that we called "Kinfolks, Cornbread & Hillbilly Women," based on our own early memories and family stories.

Sifting through those memories inevitably brought on fond recollections of the food I enjoyed as a child when I lived with my grandparents, John and Mallie Hamilton, six miles up Wooten's Creek—about twelve miles as the crow flies from Hell-fer-Sartin (Certain)—in Leslie County, from 1935 until the early 1940s.

They owned about a thousand acres, some of it virgin timberland. Pa farmed and raised cattle, but I can't recall ever eating beef. He also raised pigs, and we did eat lots of pork. Granny made sausage and there was a smokehouse at the edge of the yard with a little porch that was my playhouse in the summertime. Granny also used lard rendered from pork fat to make lye soap that she boiled up in a large black kettle in the yard.

Of course we feasted on delectable chicken that Granny had fried slowly in a cast-iron skillet. And if she happened to wring the neck of a chicken that was old and tough or fat, it went into a stew pot with tender dumplings. I remember playing with newly hatched biddies, much to the hens' consternation. I helped Granny hunt for the nests hidden by the free-ranging hens, and she left a glass nest egg after we robbed the nest, to fool the hen. Once, when I went to gather eggs, I found a blacksnake that had swallowed a nest egg and was desperately winding itself around a little tree, trying to break the glass egg. I went running for Granny, because I was deathly afraid of snakes, even the harmless ones, and she killed the poor thing to put it out of its misery.

Granny warned me to watch out for copperheads, admonishing that they hid in briar patches. She had a cousin who was immune to copperhead venom because he had been bitten so many times. I wasn't interested in challenging his record. So I was always cautious, especially around the blackberry bushes when we picked berries, although, thankfully, I never saw a single snake there.

The wild blackberries were wonderful back then, fat and sweet, and it didn't take long to fill a pail. Nowadays, the wild berries are scrawny and tart; there's no comparison. But the copperheads are still thriving in southeastern Kentucky.

The berry pickers were usually me, Granny, and any of Mom's younger brothers and sisters that Granny could induce to join us. After we filled our buckets and toted them home, Granny made a couple of cobblers, then canned the rest of the berries and stored them in the pantry. If I close my eyes I can still almost taste the sweet tang of those cobblers and feel the warm juice run down my chin. We didn't have ice cream to garnish the cobbler, but it went down easy with big swigs of fresh sweet milk cool from the well.

Before I was six, my Uncle Carl would take me along sometimes when he went squirrel hunting, for squirrel and rabbit were two wild game meats that also supplemented the Hamilton table. He would swing me up on his shoulders and I would ride there, playing horsey ("Giddy-up, Giddy-up") with my legs dangling down around his neck, and off into the woods we'd gallop. He'd put me down under a tree and go off hunting, then bring back squirrels as he bagged them, leaving them for me to proudly guard.

When I got a little older, hunting wasn't nearly as much fun: after we got home, I had to hold the hind legs of the dead squirrels while my uncle skinned them.

Occasionally, my uncles went fishing in Tennessee. That's how I learned I was allergic to fish: I was the only one who got sick after a big trout dinner.

We didn't eat beef because it was more valuable sold than slaughtered, although we certainly utilized milk and butter from our cows. But never cheese. I cannot recall ever seeing cheese served in a mountain home when I was a child. Churning butter was a tedious chore that often fell to me, and one I hated passionately. I hated both the smell and the taste of the clabbered milk that went into the churn, and somehow it seemed to always take longer for the butter to come for me than it did for anyone else.

Beans were a staple for dinner and supper, and one of the chores I helped Granny do after the green beans ripened in the summer was making shucky beans for our winter fare. That meant snapping off the ends of the beans and removing the strings, then using a big needle and sturdy thread to create long strings of beans that would be hung behind the woodstove in the kitchen to dry. This was a pioneer method of food preservation, but we liked the beans so much that after World War II started and my mother and I were living near Flagstaff, Arizona, where she worked in a munitions plant, Granny mailed us boxes of shucky beans.

No electric lines were strung up Wooten's Creek until I was a teenager. However, long before that my Uncle Dan rigged up a water wheel on the creek that generated enough electricity for lights and a radio, but we didn't have a refrigerator. In the summertime, Granny put milk and butter in a galvanized bucket and lowered them into a well in the backyard to keep cool. We drew drinking water up in a pail from a well inside the kitchen.

The nearest general store was also the post office, up Polecat Hollow, run by my great-uncle, Jack Melton, about three miles from home. My great-aunt, Becky Caudill, had a very small store in her house which was closer, and she always gave me horehound candy. I didn't like the taste much then; as an adult I like it better.

We frequently ate store-bought rice, but it was always sweetened: with milk and sugar as a cereal with breakfast, or in a pudding. The usual breads were hot biscuits for breakfast, cornbread for dinner and supper. Granny made her cornbread with white cornmeal ground from our own corn at Uncle Jack's grist mill. She baked it in a hot cast-iron skillet and never so much as whispered the word "sugar" in its presence.

To this day, a favorite comfort food of mine is what the writer James Still calls crumble-in: cornbread crumbled into a bowl of sweet milk. Of course, the milk I crumbled my bread into then was neither homogenized nor pasteurized, but straight from the cow's udder to the milk pail to our kitchen. The milk I crumble my bread into today, alas, is skim.

As I got older, Pa sometimes let me watch and even help a little when he robbed the bees. This was an elaborate production that required protective clothing and pumping smoke into the hives (he had several) to drive the bees out so he could cut away combs dripping with honey.

In the fall, Pa usually held a stiroff, set up near our patch of sugar-cane. Neighbors who came to help left with jars of syrup as payment. I always felt sorry for the mule who had to plod around and around in a circle, turning the machine that ground juice from the cane into a large vat. It was hot work, intensified by a fire under the vat boiling the molasses down. For kids, it was fun, because we cut sticks of cane and dipped them into the boiling mess and sucked off the syrup that stuck to the cane.

Pa always got upset and went around muttering that it was unsanitary, kids sticking those canes into the molasses, then in their mouths, then back in the molasses. I'd get sassy and tell him that all that boiling destroyed the germs.

Granny used molasses in lieu of sugar sometimes in cooking, particularly during the war, when sugar was rationed. One dessert that was a favorite and always contained molasses was a stack cake, a simple tier cake with spiced apples slathered between the layers. It would be stored for a day or two to "age" while the flavors blended before it was cut.

Like many mountain women, Granny did not write her recipes down (neither did Mom), so I've had to approximate them, not an easy task. My Uncle Carl and his wife Edna now live in the house in Wooten's Creek where I lived as a child, and Aunt Edna bakes a cobbler similar to Granny's, but she doesn't write down recipes either. So I got her daughter to follow her around while she was making a cobbler and write everything down, and now we have a recipe.

However, Edna's blackberries come from the garden, not from the wild berry patches. Uncle Carl planted some rows of Navajo blackberries and they are bearing well now. Those that don't go fresh into cobblers go into the freezer for winter cobblers.

Finding a stack cake recipe was more of a challenge. There are a lot of them out there, in cookbook after cookbook, but not one that I feel is exactly like Granny's. No one in the family bakes stack cakes now, but I recalled that my aunt, Harriet Hamilton McDaniel, had once plunked herself down beside a stack cake someone brought to a Farler reunion (Granny's maiden name was Farler) in Leslie County and stayed there until it was cut to make sure she got a piece.

I called Harriet. She was willing to help me attempt a stack cake, and she had stronger recall of watching Granny make one than I did.

I've found a lot of stack cake recipes, and in the process learned from the *Better Homes and Gardens Heritage Cook Book* that the stack cake was a traditional pioneer wedding cake, assembled at the celebration itself. Each guest would bring a layer, and the layers were joined together with applesauce made from fresh or dried apples, depending on the season. The bride's popularity could be gauged, it seems, by the number of stacks and layers per stack.

When Granny made stack cakes, five or six layers to a cake, she also made several oblong ginger cakes that were passed out to the children and adults standing around the table waiting, as soon as they came out of the oven. Oh, that heavenly smell that brought everybody crowding into the kitchen!

So in an effort to recreate a facsimile of Granny's stack cake, I drove to Harriet's house in Richmond, Kentucky, and we spent an afternoon concocting one using a variation of two or three recipes I had found. Harriet had scrubbed a big dishpan for use by us because she remembered Granny using one for mixing stack cakes, with a lot of flour, making a well in the center for the other ingredients. Granny mixed with her hands, Harriet recalled, rather than a spoon, until she had dough of a consistency that could be formed into balls that were then patted out into circles to make the layers.

The recipe called for two eggs, and as I broke them, Harriet kept saying, plaintively, "But Mom always used six eggs." Yes, but she was making two stack cakes and umpteen little oblong ginger goodies as well.

There was too much flour in the dishpan, but between us Harriet and I produced two rather heavy, awkward-looking stack cakes. Tasted pretty good, but not like Granny's!

But then, I wonder, can any taste match the one so fondly remembered over so many years?

Aunt Edna's Blackberry Cobbler

one cup water
one quart blackberries
two cups sugar

Combine water, blackberries, and sugar in saucepan and cook until mixture boils. Set aside.

Biscuit dough
seven heaping tablespoons self-rising flour
one cup milk
one-half cup shortening
Mix, roll out, and cut into strips.

Place berries in rectangular baking pan and heat on stove. Mix two tablespoons cornstarch and one cup water with whisk; pour into berries. Stir. Cover berries with strips of dough, criss-crossing for latticework design. Bake at 350 degrees for ten to fifteen minutes.

Granny's Stack Cake

four cups dried apples
water
one cup brown sugar
one-half teaspoon ginger
one teaspoon cinnamon
one-fourth teaspoon cloves
one-half teaspoon allspice

Put the dried apples in a heavy pan and cover with water. Cook until soft, adding water as necessary to keep apples from sticking to the pan. While the apples are still hot, mash them, and add spices.

Cake dough
four to five cups flour
one teaspoon baking soda
one-half teaspoon salt
two-thirds cup shortening
one cup sugar
one cup molasses
one cup buttermilk

two eggs, beaten
one teaspoon ginger
one teaspoon vanilla

While the apples are cooking, sift together four cups of flour, soda, and salt. Cream shortening, sugar, and molasses. Mix the buttermilk and eggs. In small, alternating amounts, add buttermilk and flour mixtures to the creamed sugar and shortening, mixing well after each addition. Use as much additional flour as needed to get consistency of biscuit dough.

Preheat oven to 350 degrees. Pat dough into ball and divide into five or six handfuls. Bake in a greased and floured pan or iron skillet, one at a time or more, if you have more than one pan. Bake approximately twenty minutes. Cool.

Spread one to one and one-half cups dried apple puree between cake layers and smooth around the sides. Wait at least one day before serving. Cut into very thin slices.

ᦥShirley Williams was born in Leslie County at Frew, Kentucky, and now lives in Louisville. She is a graduate of the Hindman Settlement School and Berea College and was a Professional Journalism Fellow at Stanford University. Now retired, she worked for the *Louisville Courier-Journal* for thirty-three years, many of those years as editor of the Sunday book page, then as a feature writer for the Accent and Arts sections, the Sunday Magazine and the Indiana edition. She has served on the faculty of various university writing workshops and the Hindman Settlement School's Appalachian Writers Workshop, and, since its inception, Williams has served as a judge of the Weatherford Award, a prize for publications that increase awareness of Appalachian culture. She and three other Louisville women with Eastern Kentucky roots —Ronni Lundy, Judi Jenkins, and Sheila Joyce—wrote a play, *Kinfolks, Cornbread and Hillbilly Women*, based on family stories, which they have performed in cities and towns across Kentucky and also in Ohio and Indiana.

Afterword

From Oats to Grits, Mutton to Pork: North British Foodways in Southern Appalachia

JIM WAYNE MILLER

Until I started leafing through the text, I had not realized how often in my autobiographical novel *Newfound* I had been concerned with *food*—the gathering, preparation, preservation, and consumption of food; with attitudes toward food; even with superstitions relating to food. When I was writing the novel I was not concerned with food, as such, in the least. Yet since food, along with clothing and shelter, is a basic necessity, it should not be surprising that so much of the story touches on food in some way. Although I did not intend the novel to do so, I see now that *Newfound* provides a quite accurate account of foodways among people of modest background in the southern Appalachians in the 1930s and 1940s, when the economy had shifted from an almost exclusively agrarian base to a mix of subsistence farming and mill, mine, and factory work.

In the opening section the narrator's father, James Wells, has quit his job at a mine and undertaken a dubious venture in cement blockmaking. Nora, the mother, is concerned about providing food for her children—the narrator, Robert, and his younger brother and sister, Eugene and Jeanette. The father has made a lot of cement blocks but hasn't sold any; his old Studebaker has locked up in reverse gear; and his blockmaking machine keeps breaking. The mother needs cash to buy some more jars and lids to can blackberries, and to make blackberry jelly and jam.

"June was as good as over and Dad hadn't sold the first block.

"Mom threw it up to him that now we had no car, and she couldn't go where the best blackberries were. The ones near the house, where she'd been picking with Jeanette and Eugene, weren't very good. But on Cook's Mountain, where her brother Clinton lived, the briers were thick and the berries were big as your thumb. We'd always gone to Uncle Clinton's toward the end of June to pick blackberries. But now we couldn't go, Mom said, and we'd have very little jelly and jam come winter, and very few canned berries for pies. And if Dad thought the store bill we'd already run up was something, she went on, then wait and see what it would be come winter. Peaches. That was another thing. She always bought peaches from the peddlers who came around. But there'd be no money this time, so we'd have no peaches, either. And Dad had fiddle-faddled around in the spring when Ed Reeves had had three litters of pigs—three litters—and we hadn't bought one, and so come fall we'd have no hog to slaughter, no ham, no shoulder meat, no sausage.

"'Will you ever wind down?' Dad asked, wild-eyed. He buttered a piece of hot cornbread and looked around the table at us children.

"Mom said she wouldn't wind down. She reminded Dad that we were eating new potatoes and green beans and tomatoes and peas and squash and okra from Grandma and Grandpa Smith's garden. Grandpa Smith came every day with a basket of this, a bucket of that. And other things we needed we were buying out of Grandpa Wells's store—on credit. Mom threw that up to him. It was the farmer who was secure, she said. The farmer always had work and food to put on the table.

"'I have work!' Dad said.

"'Um-hummmmm!' Mom said disdainfully. She recollected aloud that years ago Grandpa Wells had tried to get Dad to take over the job of running the farm, but, no, Dad had to traipse off to the mines, drive a truck, then try to go into business for himself, then go back to driving a truck for the mines. If we had stayed on the farm, we'd be well off now. It broke her heart, Mom said, after all these years, still to be living off her mama and papa—and his.

"Dad said he hadn't been cut out for a farmer, and Mom had never understood that, either. Oh, he loved the smoked ham and garden greens, he admitted, but that didn't make him a farmer.

"And it was true: green growing things seemed to wither at his touch. Once Mom had kept after him until he ordered some seedling trees to set along the edge of the yard. Not one lived. . . .

"No, Dad could stand oil and grease and coal dust, but he couldn't stand fresh-plowed dirt in his shoe-tops. I'd seen him plow a row or two of corn at Grandpa Wells's, and once or twice he'd helped out at tobacco-setting time. He never lasted long, though, and he looked little and lost standing in plowed ground."

The father's blockmaking venture finally succeeds in a qualified way: he barters cement blocks for a supply of jams, jellies, and peach preserves; for a Poland China pig and corn to feed it. He trades blocks to a local bootlegger for half-gallon jars of whiskey, which he converts to cash. But the mother's insecurity in this jerry-built economy, abetted by her husband's ongoing quixotic ventures, only increases, and finally becomes intolerable. They separate, and the following spring the mother, taking the children with her, goes to live with her tenant-farmer parents, the narrator Robert's Grandma and Grandpa Smith.

"Except for missing Dad [Robert narrates], I didn't feel I'd left home, for I had always gone back and forth between our house and Grandma and Grandpa Smith's. Bertie, Grandpa's mule; Sarah, the brindled milk cow, and Betsy, the black-and-white one; his foxhounds, Luke and Leader, Jamup and Honey; the chickens that walked poles to roost at night; the snake-headed guinea hens that screeched and pottericked when they are excited—all this was familiar to me. And Grandma Smith made us apple turnovers, let me drink coffee, and treated me more like I was a grown-up than Mom did."

Food and food preparation loom large in Robert's recollection of the first summer he lives with his grandparents:

"That summer we had tender new potatoes from the patch we'd planted, and okra and cucumbers, onions, peppers, and tomatoes from the garden. When we went with Grandma Smith to pick sweet corn, Jeanette said, "Mind your tongue in the cornfield, because there are lots of ears listening! Right, Grandma?" Grandma Smith said that was right.

"She made rhubarb pies for us. On weekends she and Mom [who has taken a job at Blue Ridge Manufacturing] canned corn and beans and tomatoes and little pint jars of chopped pickles called chow-chow. 'What's green when they're red, and ripe only when they're black?' Grandma Smith asked. 'Blackberries, of course!' Jeanette said. Grandma Smith said the blackberries were ripe, and she sent us out on the ridges and into the pasture fields to pick them. She and Mom made blackberry jam and jelly.

"In July peddlers came by with a truckload of peaches. Grandma and Mom bought several bushels and canned them. Eugene and Jeanette and I washed mason jars all summer, it seemed. After the jars came out of the pressure cooker, and before we carried them to the cool can house, they stood on shelves in the kitchen overnight. Before I went to sleep, I'd sometimes hear a jar lid go *plink*. The lids made that sound when they sealed, Mom said."

Robert's Grandpa Smith is a beekeeper. Robert describes how the old man "robs" his bees: "He stood over the bee gums wearing gloves, a long-sleeved shirt, and a wire cage over his head. He puffed smoke from his bee smoker on the bees to stun them and frighten them away. Eugene ate some of the honey while it was still warm, although Grandma Smith warned him not to, and the honey made him sick. I got too close to the gums and an angry bee buzzed my head, got tangled in my hair, and when I tried to slap it away, it stung me right on top of my head.

"Mom, Jeanette, and Grandma Smith stayed in the house with the doors closed until Grandpa had finished taking the racks of honey from the gums. Then they cut the golden honey out of the racks and stored it in jars. Grandma Smith said she probably should have come outside and allowed herself to get stung on the hand, because a bee sting was good for arthritis. The jars of honey were a smoky blond color next to the yellow peaches on the shelves in the can house. We had honey with buttered biscuits for breakfast, and that August Mom and Jeanette used some honey in a birthday cake for Grandma Smith."

Grandma Smith's notion that a bee sting is good for her arthritis is but one of her many beliefs and superstitions. She has a saying for conjuring warts, one for "drawing" fire from a burn, another for making butter, and she knows what to do when a swarm of Grandpa Smith's bees threaten to fly away: "Grandma Smith knew spells to make butter come, and when she had Eugene and me take turns working the dasher up and down in the wooden churn, she taught us rhymes to say that would make the flecks of butter appear in the buttermilk.

"She knew things about honeybees. Grandpa Smith had five beehives—he called them 'bee gums'—and one day when we were working in the garden and Grandpa Smith was off helping Coy Marler, Grandma Smith dropped her hoe and ran toward the house as fast as she could. I looked in the direction she had looked, and saw that a great dark cloud of bees was rising from one of the bee gums. Grandma Smith came back out of the house with a pie pan and a big spoon, and she ran along under the slowly moving cloud of bees, beating the pie pan with a spoon. She followed them far down into the pasture below the garden, still beating the pie pan, where the swarm settled on the limb of a jack pine. The bees were so heavy they made the limb droop toward the ground, like a branch weighted down with snow in winter. Then she sent me to find Grandpa. When he came he brought another bee gum from the barn, cut the whole limb off the tree with his pocket knife, and carried the swarm of bees to the new gum. Reaching into the clump of bees with his bare hand, he found the queen, coaxed her into the new gum, and finally the whole swarm followed her into their new home."

Grandma Smith, as Robert tells it, is also particular about the way she gathers guinea eggs: "I went to the woods with Grandma Smith to hunt for guinea nests. (Guineas were bad about stealing their nests away, she said.) On hot afternoons we'd stand by fence rows and cow trails listening for half-wild guineas screeching after they laid eggs in nests they'd hidden in thickets, scrub pines, and chinquapins. And when we'd find a nest, Grandma Smith wouldn't take the eggs from it with her bare hand; she carried her little garden hoe, and she'd reach into the nest with the hoe and carefully roll the eggs out, one at a time, always leaving one, so the guinea would continue to lay eggs there."

The picture that emerges from Robert's descriptions of life with his maternal grandparents is that of a subsistence farm in a particular time and place, which is also typical of many parts of rural America before and after: "We didn't buy as many groceries out of the store after we moved to Grandma and Grandpa Smith's. They raised almost all their food. There were potatoes stored in a big cone-shaped mound, beneath straw. We had dried apples, ham and sausage from the smokehouse, and vegetables fresh from the garden or canned. Grandma Smith had a can house that was dug back into the side of the hill. It was always cool in summer and warm in winter. She raised two rows of popcorn in the garden, and Eugene, Jeanette, and I popped popcorn on the woodstove in the living room.

"In early spring, when pussy willows were budding along the branch bank, Mom went with us to gather cresses. She said she had gathered cresses on that same branch bank when she was a little girl. She made a salad from the cresses that tasted better than the lettuce we used to get from the store.

"Grandma Smith wanted to plant potatoes on Good Friday, but Grandpa Smith didn't have the ground quite ready, so we planted potatoes the next day. Grandma Smith said Good Friday was the best time to plant. Good Saturday was close enough, Grandpa Smith said. Eugene, Jeanette, and I helped. Mom stayed in the house and typed things she'd brought home from work. Grandma Smith showed us how to recognize the seed potatoes' 'eyes,' and how to cut them up so that each piece had an eye. The piece of potato wouldn't sprout and make a plant, she said, unless it had an eye.

"'If they have eyes, can they see?' Jeanette said.

"Grandma Smith said potatoes had eyes but they couldn't see. Neither could a needle, and a needle had an eye.

"'A shoe's got a tongue, but it can't talk,' Eugene said. He drew eyebrows over two eyes of a potato, and a mouth and nose, and held it up for us to see. Jeanette had to draw a potato face, too.

"After Grandpa Smith had the potato patch laid off in rows, we each took a row, carrying a pail of cut-up seed potatoes, and walked along dropping the pieces into the furrow about a foot apart. We stepped on each piece, pressing it down into the loose soil. Then Grandpa came along with Bertie hitched to a plow and covered the potatoes in the furrow."

Robert describes how, that fall, they harvest the potatoes and how they are "holed" in a cone-shaped mound (mentioned above). In this section Jeanette is preoccupied with plans for a birthday party, and more careless than usual: "Grandpa Smith had plowed up the whole potato patch. You could look down the rows and see the potatoes turned up in the warm afternoon sun. Grandma and Grandpa Smith and Mom were out in the patch gathering potatoes. Mom got us each a basket and set us to helping.

"Working in the row beside me, Jeanette started to worry that Grandma Wells might not have any cake or muffins when we went down there on Wednesday for the birthday party. Maybe we ought to make a cake and take it down there with us, just to make sure we had one. We could hide it in the rosebushes and go in first, and *then* go out a few minutes later and bring it in.

"'You're missin' a lot of 'em,' Eugene told Jeanette. 'You can't always see 'em. You have to stir the dirt around.' He reached over into Jeanette's row, raked through the loose dirt with his hand, and turned up a big, fat potato. 'Look!' he said. Then he uncovered another. 'Look!'

"But Jeanette was preoccupied with Grandpa Wells's birthday party. When she tried to get Grandma Smith to help her bake a cake, Grandma Smith said, 'Why, there's half a cake right there in the pie safe.'"

"Mom heard them talking about cake, thought Jeanette was wanting to eat cake before supper, and said Jeanette couldn't have any.

"Jeanette said she meant a cake for Wednesday.

"'She's not finding nearly all of 'em!' Eugene said. Exasperated with Jeanette, he uncovered another potato she had missed. 'Somebody might as well just do her row over!'

"Grandma Smith said she didn't know what Jeanette was talking about—a cake for Wednesday? So Jeanette explained the whole thing: how next Wednesday was Grandpa Wells's birthday and we had already got him some gifts and hidden them in the house and we were going to go over there and surprise him.

"Grandma Smith's right hand went up to the side of her weathered face, the way it always did when she was surprised.

"Mom looked dubious at first. But it turned out she thought Jeanette was talking about a birthday cake for Grandma Wells. [Robert's mother never got along with her mother-in-law.] When she understood Jeanette wanted to bake a cake for Grandpa Wells, not Grandma Wells, she said that would be all right.

"Mom, Jeanette, and Grandma Smith went to the house to start supper, leaving Eugene, Grandpa Smith, and me to hole up the potatoes for winter. We knew how to do it, for we'd helped do it last fall, too. Grandpa Smith said we had so many potatoes this year, we'd have to do two potato holes, so we dug two shallow depressions in the ground at the edge of the potato patch. We carried the baskets of potatoes and gently dumped them into the two depressions, piling them up until there were two cone-shaped mounds. We covered the mounds with straw from the barn loft, then, working with shovels, tossed dirt on the straw mounds. At the bottom of each mound Grandpa Smith placed a short length of stovepipe that extended beyond the dirt, but back through the straw to the potatoes. Finishing up, we stuffed the stovepipes tight with straw. Now when the cold weather came and we needed potatoes, we could remove the straw, reach into the pipe, and pull the potatoes out, one or two at a time. And as we used them up, others would roll down into their place."

There were no chestnuts to be gathered in the fall. The great chestnut trees had been killed by a blight earlier in the century. Robert hears stories from his grandparents about how abundant the chestnuts were when they were growing up, but now chestnut trees stood, grey skeletons, in the woods. But a chestnut-like nut called the chinquapin grows on shrubby bushes and can be gathered when the prickly burrs burst open:

"Fall came, and we started to school again. . . . In the afternoons when we came home from school, and before we did chores, Eugene, Jeanette, and I picked chinquapins on the ridges above Grandma and Grandpa Smith's. We ate chinquapins, cracking the soft black hulls with our teeth, then turning the nut out of the hull with our tongues, until the tips of our tongues were sore. Jeanette made a necklace by stringing the shiny black chinquapins on fishing line with a big needle."

In autumn they also gathered walnuts and helped make molasses: "Fall came. Leaves turned yellow and blazing red and began to rattle in the wind. The air turned crisp. . . . We gathered walnuts and got our hands stained yellow from the walnut hulls.

"We also helped Grandpa Smith and Coy Marler and Jess Woody make molasses. Grandpa Smith hitched Bertie to a long pole on the molasses mill, and Bertie walked around and around, turning the mill, pressing the sweet juice from the cane. Eugene tasted the dark syrup that remained after the juice had been boiled; it didn't make him sick the way the honey had."

Late autumn is also the time for hog slaughtering: "Just before Thanksgiving Grandpa Smith slaughtered the largest of the three hogs in the big pen out by the barn. Coy Marler came to help. They hung the hog on a gambrel stick with a rope that worked on a pulley suspended from a tree limb. They lowered the hog into a big barrel of steaming water, raised it again, and scraped off the loose hair. Soon the hog was hams and shoulders and sausage in the smokehouse, and Eugene had the hog's bladder for a balloon."

The Newfound grade school, which they had always attended, is closed, and Robert and his brother and sister, Eugene and Jeanette, begin attending West Madison Consolidated. Robert misses the old school: "West Madison was very modern, bright and colorful. There were skylights in the rooms and halls; smooth tiled floors, which the janitors swept with green sawdust; pink, yellow, and green rooms; desks arranged in a semicircle around the teacher's; green writing boards and yellow chalk. But I longed for Newfound School, with its old desks bolted to the oil-soaked floor, and the huge oak tree in the yard, scarred with everyone's initials."

Miss Hudspeth, a nurse at the new school, makes Robert, an eighth grader now, self-conscious about who he is, where he lives, and even about the food he eats: "Miss Hudspeth was relentless. The students from Newfound became her pet project. She had been a missionary in Central America, and I suppose we reminded her of the diseased, undernourished children she had known there. We shocked her with our ignorance, our backwardness, and our poverty in the midst of the splendor of West Madison. She disapproved of our sack lunches. 'For only pennies a day, you can have a hot, nourishing meal,' she would say. 'Be sure to tell your fathers and mothers.'

"When Miss Hudspeth brought just us students from Newfound together for a lecture, we at least enjoyed a kind of privacy in which to feel ashamed of ourselves. But usually we were scattered among the others, especially when she showed films in the darkened gym. One of these films was called 'The Wheel of Good Health' and showed healthy, happy children eating fresh fruits, green leafy vegetables, yellow vegetables, cheese, milk, fish, poultry, and all the rest, maintaining all the while, in spite of the constant chewing, expressions of pure delight. A recurring wheel showed the basic seven daily requirements for good nutrition.

"When the film ended, Miss Hudspeth motioned for the lights to be turned on, stood out on the gym floor with her hands clasped together, and talked to us about our personal diets. She asked several students what they had for breakfast that morning, and they recited: bacon, eggs, toast, milk, cereal—all the lovely, approved things.

"'What about you little Newfound folk?' she asked, pointing to my brother Eugene, who was sitting on the front row of bleachers looking up at her. Eugene always listened as if his life depended on it, but he never realized how backward he was. 'You, little brown-eyes,' Miss Hudspeth said, 'What did you eat for breakfast?'

"Eugene started rocking back and forth nervously, and gripping his jeans at the knees. 'Biscuits,' he said, his voice sounding unusually high and thin in the gym; '. . . and sawmill gravy,' he continued, in the singsong of recitation. I could see Miss Hudspeth was shocked, as no doubt she knew she would be, for she smiled ever more fiercely, and pointed to another child. But Eugene was not through reciting. '. . .and molasses,' he intoned, 'new molasses!'

"A half-mad, hysterical laugh rose to the high ceiling of the gym and bounced back before I realized that it was I who had laughed. I cringed down . . . and looked to see whether anyone on either side of me knew that Eugene was my brother."

The references to food in this growing-up novel, Newfound, are by no means exhaustive. In addition to those fruits and vegetables mentioned, our gardens also produced pumpkins, squash, turnips, parsnips, radishes, okra, cucumbers, asparagus, peppers (sweet and hot), and in addition to ordinary tomatoes, the small cherry tomatoes which we called tommytoes. I mentioned corn in the novel, but not the golden ears of young garden corn, or sweet corn, which, boiled and served and eaten with butter and salt, are of course roasting ears, which we pronounced something like "roasenears." And with respect to wild things, in addition to picking blackberries, cresses, and chinquapins, we gathered hickory nuts, wild grapes (called fox grapes), and poke (for poke sallet, as my grandmother called it). In the spring, for the stout of heart, there were ramps, something like wild onions but with a more powerful, garlic-like odor. My grandfather taught me to eat ramps chopped up in scrambled eggs.

We also ate wild game: rabbits caught in deadfalls or rabbit "gums" (called Hoover boxes in the Depression) or shot on rabbit hunts; squirrels, partridges, and mountain grouse, which we called pheasants, though they were not the ring-necked variety. Occasionally we had venison and bear, and some folks ate possums and coons. From the French Broad River we had black bass and catfish, and from North and South Turkey and Big and Little Sandy Mush creeks, suckers, which we caught not with hook and line but by "grabbling," which was done by wading the creeks and feeling back under banks and catching the fish with our hands. (I recollect that when my grandmother would remove one or two tender, young potatoes from beneath each potato plant in a garden row, digging them out with a claw-like utensil, then pushing the dirt back, leaving the other potatoes to grow to maturity, she also called this "grabbling" potatoes.) Grabbling in the creeks was usually a communal activity: a dozen or more men and older boys would wade upstream, tossing their catch up onto the bank to younger boys who carried wet burlap sacks to hold the fish. In early spring white suckers ran up the creeks in schools, much like salmon, and were so numerous that it was not unusual for a group of men and boys to catch dozens of them within a few hours. These fish, averaging a foot long, were cleaned and served up at fish fries usually conducted by the fishermen themselves. These fish fries were often outdoor affairs where whiskey was an obligatory accompaniment.

The only domestic animals slaughtered in *Newfound* are hogs. There is mention of hams, shoulders, and sausage in connection with the slaughter. But hog killing also provided us with a prepared food we called liver mush, which could be fried and served like pork sausage. And what remained after fat was "rendered" for lard were crisp bits not unlike pieces of pork rind, called "cracklins," which were added to a mixture of cornmeal, eggs, and milk (or buttermilk) to make "cracklin bread."

Though it is not mentioned in the novel, some people in the New-found community slaughtered cattle. Typically, a farmer would slaughter a "beef," keep part of it for his family's needs, and give the rest to relatives and neighbors, or peddle the remainder, door-to-door. I know of no one in the southern Appalachian mountains, the setting of *Newfound*, who raised sheep. Consequently, no one ate mutton. But during World War II, when there was rationing of many foodstuffs, my father, the model for James Wells, the father in *Newfound*, raised goats (one of his many enter-prises) and occasionally slaughtered one for our table—always after we children (and our mother, too, for that matter) had come to think of the goat as a pet.

Just like James Wells and his wife Nora in *Newfound*, my father and mother were very different people, almost opposites in their views, tastes, and preferences. My mother was conservative and traditional, reluctant to try new things, new foods among them. (Her brother, home from World War II, where he served in Italy as an army cook, introduced her with some difficulty to Worcestershire sauce.) She did not approve of goats as a source of food for the table—because no one else she knew ate goats! She held a number of superstitious beliefs about foods and combinations of foods, her authority for these beliefs based vaguely on some Old Testa-ment food law, or a confused, handed-down version of one of those re-strictions. For example, she believed that eating fish and drinking sweet milk at the same meal could prove fatal. My father delighted in demon-strating to her, by eating fried fish, drinking milk, and suffering no ill consequences, that her notion was just foolish. But she held firm to her belief in the face of the evidence. (My mother had also learned from her mother to refer to milk that had spoiled as "blinked." The term is said to derive from the belief that a mischievous supernatural creature from the realm of fairies, gnomes, and leprechauns could spoil milk by giving it a version of the "evil eye.")

My father was always affronting my mother with some new food he'd bring unexpectedly from Asheville—usually some variety of seafood. He brought home the first oysters we ever ate, the first shrimp, clams, and lobster. My mother would shrink back from such exotica, professing she wouldn't touch them. Besides, she didn't have the slightest idea how to prepare them. No matter. My father would swing into action and be-come chef, frying up oysters or shrimp or whatever with supreme confi-dence and great exuberance—and making a huge mess in the kitchen.

I have naturally inherited the foodways of my parents and grandparents, and of the community in which I grew up. My tastes, attitudes, and preferences with regard to food are in some ways like my mother's, conservative and traditional. I like green beans heavily seasoned in the old-fashioned country manner and surely overcooked, like the roasts. Like my mother, I don't automatically gravitate to every trendy thing that comes down the pike. Like her, I am perfectly happy even without a crock pot, a wok, or a microwave oven. (A wok, though, has much to recommend it!)

But I am also my father's son and not afraid to try something different. And my grandfather's grandson. I can whip up a passable scrambled eggs and ramps. I love every sort of seafood, but prefer fried to baked, broiled, or boiled. This is a regional preference, not just a family heritage. Early travelers in southern Appalachia remarked on the tendency of the people to fry everything. David Hackett Fischer, in his book *Albion's Seed*, says southern highland cooking reflects its north British origins. Foodways in the southern highlands, according to Fischer, are to some degree a product of frontier traditions, but "mainly they are an expression of the folk customs that had been carried from the borders of north Britain. Strong continuities appeared in favored foodstuffs, in methods of cooking and also in the manner of eating." The presence or absence in the southern highlands of certain foods and foodways is explained, Fischer maintains, by the blend of frontier conditions and cultural continuity with north Britain. In some respects, southern highland foodways necessarily departed from the customs of north Britain. Oats yielded to maize, which was pounded into cornmeal and cooked by boiling. But this was merely a change from oatmeal mush to cornmeal mush, or "grits" as it was called in the southern highlands. The ingredients changed, but the texture of the dish remained the same.

Another change occurred in the consumption of meat. The people of north Britain had rarely eaten pork at home. Pigs' flesh was as loathsome to the borderers as it had been to the children of Abraham and Allah. But that taboo did not survive in the New World, where sheep were difficult to maintain and swine multiplied even more rapidly than the humans who fed upon them. Pork rapidly replaced mutton on backcountry tables, but it continued to be boiled and fried in traditional border ways.

New American vegetables also appeared on backcountry tables. Most families kept a "truck-patch," in which they raised squashes, cushaws (a relative of squash), pumpkins, gourds, beans, and sweet roasting ears of

Indian corn. Many families also raised "sallet" greens, cress, poke, and bear's lettuce. Here again, the ingredients were new, but the consumption of "sallet" and "greens" were much the same as in the old country.

Everything Fischer describes comports well with the foodways of my southern highland community, which I call Newfound. His mention of the change from the oatmeal mush of north Britain to the cornmeal mush of the New World reminds me that Big and Little Sandy Mush creeks in my community are so named because settlers, taking water from the creek to prepare a meal, got sand in their cornmeal mush.

I may be typical of my time and place in that I learned my few culinary skills not from my mother, or grandmother, but from my father and grandfather and from hunting and fishing cronies. Like wilted (or "killed") cabbage and sausage. This dish, like the few other things I can prepare, is surely not something you'd invite people to, but it suits my taste, and the taste of people who would be present when I prepare it. The same goes for fried fish and hushpuppies, which can be as tasty as hot dogs at a picnic or baseball game.

The way I learned to prepare fish (certainly nothing out of the ordinary) I learned creekside, or camped by the French Broad River, where we caught catfish on trotlines. You need a brown paper bag, some cornmeal, milk, eggs, cooking oil, and a frying pan. Dredge filets of fish through a bowl of milk into which you have beaten a couple of eggs. Toss a couple of cups of cornmeal into the paper bag, and on top of the meal three or four filets. Shake the filets inside the bag until they are covered with cornmeal. Then place them in a frying pan in which you have already heated the oil. (You can heat the frying pan over a camp stove, small woodfire between two rocks, over charcoal—whatever. When you have fried all the filets, mix the cornmeal you have dusted them with into the bowl of milk-and-egg mixture. Make hushpuppies out of this mixture, adding chopped peppers, onions, anything you think would be good or that is available. If the cooking oil is deep enough, make the hushpuppies round; if not, then flat.

This kind of food and its preparation will strike many people as laughably crude and primitive, which reminds me that an important ingredient in this food, its preparation and consumption, is an attitude—a combination of my father's confidence (despite experience or skill!) and willingness to improvise. A part of this attitude, too, is the notion that you eat the food because it is good, not because it is good for you. Food is not medicine, a class marker, or a badge of discrimination (though food may be all these things to some people). I certainly no longer feel apologetic about or ashamed of any food, as does Robert in *Newfound* when his little brother recites what he ate for breakfast. I do not assume, as Robert did, that the humble fare carried from home to school was automatically inferior to "store-bought" foods, or food served in the school cafeteria. And I notice that in recent years such simple fare—ham, sausage, and steak biscuits, sometimes served with milk gravy—has become popular in fast food franchises. At the same time we are surrounded by food fads that I can only understand as the result of some mass hysteria. I am reminded of Jack Sharkey's reworking of the nursery rhyme: "Jack Sprat could eat no fat, / His wife could eat no lean. A real sweet pair of neurotics." Food should not be a religion, either, though it may be the culmination of a ritual, such as a hunting or a fishing trip. A part of my mostly inherited attitude toward food is also qualified agreement with the notion that you are what you eat: no, you're not exactly what you eat, but still there is a resemblance. And not just what you eat, but how you eat, and even how you cook tells a lot about you.

Jim Wayne Miller

ᖴJim Wayne Miller (1936-1996)who grew up in Leicester, North Carolina. He received his B.A. in English from Berea College and his Ph.D. in German from Vanderbilt University. For thirty-three years he taught German at Western Kentucky University while also publishing six collections of poetry, literary criticism, German translations into English, one play, and two novels. Miller's best-known works include *Copperhead Cane* (poetry), *The More Things Change the More They Stay the Same* (ballads), *Dialogue with a Dead Man* (poetry), *The Mountains Have Come Closer* (poetry), *Vein of Words* (poetry), *Brier & His Book* (poetry), *Newfound* (novel), and *His First, Best Country* (novel). The setting of almost all of Miller's writing, Appalachia, also served as the region of his U.S. literary expertise. For many years he taught creative writing at conferences and workshops throughout Kentucky, especially at the Hindman Settlement School's Appalachian Writers Workshop, and he served on the advisory board of Green River Writers, Inc. In 1996 Miller, who resided in Bowling Green, Kentucky, died of lung cancer at age fifty-nine. His survivors include his wife, Mary Ellen, and their three adult children.